Understanding Autism in the Early Years

Understanding Autism in the Early Years

Prithvi Perepa

Open University Press

Open University Press
McGraw-Hill Education
McGraw-Hill House
Shoppenhangers Road
Maidenhead
Berkshire
England
SL6 2QL

email: enquiries@openup.co.uk
world wide web: www.openup.co.uk

and Two Penn Plaza, New York, NY 10121-2289, USA

First published 2013

A catalogue record of this book is available from the British Library

ISBN-13: 978-0-335-24664-9
ISBN-10: 0-335-24664-8
eISBN: 978-0-335-24665-6

Library of Congress Cataloging-in-Publication Data
CIP data applied for

Typeset by Aptara, Inc.

Praise for this book

"This is a timely and very practical book addressed to all those working in early years settings who are working with, or who will be working with, children on the autism spectrum (i.e. all staff in any early years setting). It gives clear and authoritative information on current understanding of the autism spectrum, and draws on a wide range of literature to do so, while being written in a clear direct style that should be accessible to all. It would also be of benefit to family members who want to understand their child and how to best work with the systems and services they encounter. The book is realistic about the challenges but is also full of practical positive suggestions which respect the contribution of all to enabling effective practice: staff in the early years setting, support services, the family and, not least, the children themselves."

Professor Rita Jordan BSc.MSc.MA.PhD.C.Psychol.AFBPS.OBE, Emeritus Professor in Autism Studies, University of Birmingham, UK

"Early years practitioners are absolutely vital partners in recognising autism and in adjusting their practice in response to the needs of children with autism. The impact they can make on families and outcomes for children is immeasurable, therefore a book like this which gives a mixture of practical strategies underpinned by evidence is a wonderful tool.

With a prevalence rate of 1 in 100 all early years practitioners will encounter young children with autism in their careers. The difference they can make by being able to recognise the condition, support families and adapt their practice is immeasurable. This clear and easy to read book will be a real boon to all early years practitioners."

Carol Povey, Director of the Centre for Autism, National Autistic Society

"Understanding Autism in the Early Years *is a clearly written and very useful book. Early years practitioners will find it helpful for recognising the signs of autism spectrum conditions in young children, working with families, and adapting their practice in ways that will help those they care for learn and develop."*

Dr Mitzi Waltz, Senior Lecturer in Autism, Sheffield Hallam University, UK

To my Mum & Dad

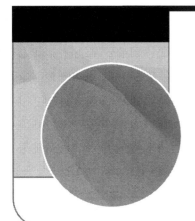

Contents

Introduction to autism spectrum

Whether you have worked with children for a long time or you are entirely new to the field you must have heard about autism spectrum disorder (ASD). It is a phrase that is getting very familiar thanks to the media interest in the subject. However, the familiarity of the term is also producing misunderstanding and contradictory information about the subject. This chapter aims to provide an introduction to the condition by stating some of the basic facts.

Autism spectrum disorder (ASD) is a term used to cover a range of difficulties in two main areas of development. The term usually means difficulty in:

- social communication and interaction, and
- imagination and flexible thinking skills.

Until recently, the areas of communication and social interaction were considered as separate and the term 'triad of impairments' was used to describe these three areas of difficulty, as suggested by Wing (1981). However, there are proposals for change in the diagnostic criteria, which will result in combining these two areas in the new *Diagnostic Statistical Manual of Mental Health Disorders* (DSM) edition V.

Autism spectrum is described as a developmental disorder. This means that it affects an individual during childhood. Hence, the symptoms are usually evident by 3 years of age, and this is indeed part of the current diagnostic criteria for both the International Classification of Diseases and Related Health Problems (ICD-10) published by the World Health Organization (2007) and the DSM-IV-TR published by the American Psychiatric Association (2000). Having said that, diagnosing children at such an early age is not always possible, especially for those with severe learning disabilities or with no associated learning difficulties. Let us look at two children to get an idea of how autism impacts on them.

Case study 1

Mohamud's mother was worried that something was different about her son when he did not like being cuddled as a baby. Then he had not started speaking by the age of 3. Even now, at 5, he hardly speaks. Sometimes he says random words, but often not to make requests. Mohamud does not like it when anything changes from his daily routine, such as going to a different park, taking a different route to the supermarket, or when friends and family visit their place. On such occasions Mohamud gets upset and starts crying and pushing the guests out.

Case study 2

At 5 years old Ben plays the piano as well as a professional. Both his parents are amazed as neither of them are musicians. He started playing when the family went to visit some relatives who had a piano and he heard them playing. It is hard to guess that Ben has any difficulties when observing him playing the piano. It can only be guessed when he is asked to stop playing before he decides he has finished, or when he decides to use the piano in the church or someone's house and he is asked not to. Ben then gets upset and shows his distress by crying and usually throwing himself on the floor. Ben's parents are not sure whether this is because they are not strict parents and he is their only son.

At first glance it may appear that these children have different abilities, but both of them have been diagnosed as being on the autism spectrum. The reason the word 'spectrum' is used is because of this disparity in the way it affects different individuals.

The discovery of autism spectrum

The idea of autism as a separate condition was developed in the early 1940s by two different professionals in two parts of the world. Leo Kanner was a child psychiatrist working in the USA and Hans Asperger was a paediatrician who lived in Austria. Leo Kanner coined the term 'early infantile autism' in 1943, based on his work with a group of 11 children. Although Hans Asperger also wrote a paper called 'Autistic psychopathies in childhood' in 1944, his work was not known to the English-speaking world until it was mentioned by Wing in an article of 1981 and later translated into English by Frith (1991). Asperger syndrome as a subcategory of autism was recognized only after this period.

Not having a separate category until the 1940s does not mean that autism did not exist before this time. In fact, there is evidence and hypothesis to identify many people who in hindsight could be described as being on the autism spectrum (Frith 2003). What this does mean is that until this time a child exhibiting difficulties in these areas would not have been diagnosed with autism.

Kanner and Asperger both believed that the children they were working with had above average intelligence. As our understanding about autism increased it became clear that this is not always the case and that some children with autism can and do have learning difficulties. Children who are diagnosed with high-functioning autism (HFA), Asperger syndrome or atypical autism may have average intelligence. It needs to be understood that children on the autism spectrum, just like any other child, may have other, additional disabilities such as learning difficulties, epilepsy, or a visual or hearing impairment as well as mental health issues. Having more than one condition is sometimes referred to as 'co-morbidity'.

How similar are autism and Asperger syndrome?

Children diagnosed with autism or Asperger syndrome both have difficulties in the above two areas, and are considered to be on the autism spectrum. The main difference between autism and Asperger syndrome was originally based on whether or not there was any delay in the development of speech. A child diagnosed with Asperger syndrome was considered to have no delay in speech development before the age of 3, and no learning difficulties. However, over the years there has been a lot of discussion among the professionals as to whether Asperger syndrome is different from high-functioning autism. There are now plans to remove the diagnostic label of Asperger syndrome as a separate subcategory from the new version of DSM.

The ideas and information provided in this book will be applicable for any child diagnosed with autism or Asperger syndrome. It will also be useful for understanding children on the autism spectrum with other diagnostic labels, such as Kanner's autism, high-functioning autism, atypical autism, pervasive developmental disorder (PDD) and pervasive developmental disorder – not otherwise specified (PDD-NOS). Children with all these labels show difficulties in similar areas, and as an early years practitioner you can use the information in this book to help any of these children and their families. Recently, some professionals have started using the term autism spectrum conditions (ASC). This term is preferred by some adults on the autism spectrum as they do not consider themselves to have a disorder, while some other people like to describe themselves as having ASD. Because of the emotional value attached to the terminology, it is important that you use the term that is comfortable to the family you are working with. I will be using 'autism' or 'autism spectrum' in this book to represent all these labels, to make it easy for reading and to avoid confusion.

Social communication and interaction

The term autism was based on the Greek word 'autos' meaning self. It was considered that children with autism were happy to be by themselves and hence the term was coined. Although this may be true in some cases, it is now understood that autism does not necessarily mean a desire to be alone. Some children with autism may want to interact with others but may not have the appropriate skills or may not understand how to start an interaction.

Social interaction requires understanding of social norms and other people's interests, and appropriate communication skills. It has been noted that children with autism have difficulty in understanding other people and anticipating their actions. One theory that is used to explain this inability to understand others is lack of theory of mind (Baron-Cohen et al. 1985), which will be looked at in detail in a later chapter.

Inability to understand others' intentions and emotions can impact on children's ability to play and interact with others as well as understand the unspoken social rules. This can mean that sometimes children with autism may come across as rude or naughty, and are unfairly judged because of their difficulties. It is important that children are helped to develop the appropriate social skills so that they are able to participate in society as much or as little as they wish.

The other important area for social interaction is communication. Communication does not just mean our ability to speak, but also using gestures, facial expressions or written information to express ourselves to others and to be able to understand other people. Children diagnosed with autism may have varying levels of communication skills. While some children, like Mohamud, may have very little speech or none at all, others may be able to speak well. However, having the ability to speak does not necessarily mean that the child will be able to communicate. Some children with well-developed speech may still find it difficult to understand simple gestures such as a head movement to say no. Similarly, they may have difficulty in initiating a conversation or making a request. It should be remembered, then, that development of speech in autism does not necessarily lead to development of communication skills. Some other common patterns that are observed in children with autism are that they may repeat what has been said to them. Some children find it difficult to use the correct pronouns or understand indirect language such as using the phrase 'can you do some drawing?' as a request. Children with autism may consider this as a genuine question and answer with yes or no.

It has also been noticed that children with autism may have difficulty in joint attention such as following finger pointing or eye gaze. Some children may also have difficulty in taking turns in games, activities or conversations. Again, with appropriate strategies, some of these skills can be taught to children with autism in their entirety, or alternative strategies can be used.

Differences in imagination and play

One of the areas you may come across often in an early years setting is the difference in play of a child with autism. Children with autism may find it more difficult to engage in pretend play or play that involves interaction with other children. This is often due to their difficulties in social interaction and communication. As a result, they may choose to play on their own, or try and engage other children in games in an unusual way. For example, a child may knock down the blocks of a tower made by another child to start a game. This may not be uncommon in other children as well, but the main difference is that a child with autism may find it difficult to judge whether his actions are causing distress to the other child.

Some children with autism may also use toys in an unconventional way. For example, rather than pushing a car the child may just hold the car in his hand and flick the wheel. Or they may sort the utensils in the toy cooking set on the basis of their colour rather than pretending to be mummy and cook. This does not mean that children with autism do not have any pretend play at all; some children are able to engage in pretend play, although this may be mostly imitated pretend play from a familiar story.

Difficulty in imagination and the inability to think flexibly could mean that children with autism may like activities which are factual and use concrete materials. Therefore, some of them may have difficulty engaging in situations such as a storytelling session. They may also find it difficult to cope with unexpected changes such as having to play indoors because of rain, or having to take a different route to the park because of roadworks.

Of course, children with autism can differ from each other, just like any other child. All children with autism will not show exactly the same behaviours. We will discuss the diagnostic criteria in more detail in the next chapter.

Prevalence and causes

It is currently assumed that there are similar rates of prevalence in all ethnic and cultural groups, although differences in prevalence rates among different countries and between different ethnic groups have been noted by some studies (Goodman and Richards 1995; Croen et al. 2002). This is an area which needs to be explored further, as the current studies do not take this into consideration. The first prevalence study by Lotter (1966) estimated that there are four cases of autism in every 10,000 people. The figures have changed since then, with various different estimates being offered. The current rate of prevalence is suggested to be about one child in every hundred being on the autism spectrum (Baird et al. 2006; Baron-Cohen et al. 2009).

Researchers are not entirely sure whether this represents a genuine increase in numbers or whether it is a result of increased awareness of the condition and better diagnostic procedures. Wing (1996) and Kielinen et al. (2000), for example, suggest that the increase in the number of children diagnosed with autism is because of wider diagnostic criteria which led to more children being diagnosed with Asperger syndrome and atypical autism. Wing (1996) and Bishop et al. (2008) suggest that, as a result of improved diagnostic tools and a broadening definition, more professionals are using the diagnostic label of autism spectrum instead of other conditions such as global learning difficulties. Not everyone considers these as possible reasons, and other areas such as environmental impact are being explored as a possible cause.

It is believed that there are more males affected by autism than females. The figures range from one female for every four males to one for every ten (MRC 2001). This difference on the basis of gender has sometimes been attributed to the genetic nature of the condition. However, Attwood et al. (2006) suggested that the difference could be the result of the way autism presents itself in females, which can make it difficult to identify. For example, they suggest that females may have greater empathy and different kinds of obsessions which may not be identified as autism using the current diagnostic tools. There is an increased interest in girls with autism, and trials are being conducted to modify the diagnostic tools to be more gender sensitive.

In spite of autism being identified as a separate condition for almost 70 years, the exact cause of the condition is still unknown. In the past, parents were often blamed as the cause of their child's autism by some professionals, such as Bettelheim (1967). However, this has been disproved and we now know that poor parenting does not cause autism. The current research points towards a neurobiological basis for the condition which is perhaps based on genetic links and brain development (MRC 2001). The main studies looking at genetic links are based on identical twins, where it has been found that if one of the twins has autism, there is high likelihood that the other twin may also have it (Bailey et al. 1995). As identical twins have the same genetic structure it is hypothesized that genes could be responsible for autism. Other sibling and family studies (Gillberg 1991; Piven et al. 1997) also seem to support this theory of autism features being more prevalent in some families. In fact, Rutter (2005) has stated that autism is one of the most heritable conditions. Pennington (2009) agrees with the view that there is a possible heritability of the condition but cautions that this cannot be linked to a single gene. This is true as we are nowhere near identifying a single 'autism gene'. Others such as Abraham and Geschwind (2008) query the genetic theory and argue that this only explains the cause in a minority of cases, and that other causes need to be explored.

There are also a number of studies which are looking at the brain development in people with autism. In a study by Courchesne (2004) it was found that children with autism have a larger brain volume, heavier brain weight and bigger head circumference than typically developing children. Elder et al. (2008) found that this large size is typically evident at one year and is usually followed by slower brain growth, leading to similar brain size as typical children by the time brain development is complete. It has been argued that this rapid development may influence the way the brain networks, and can impact specific areas such as speech and understanding emotions. However, differences in the brain may not always lead to deficits, as found in Ashwin et al.'s (2007) study which found that in people with autism different areas in the brain were compensating for understanding emotions. Therefore it is not easy to attribute all the differences found in autism to brain development or abnormality alone.

Other environmental causes are also being researched as possible triggers or causes of autism. Frith (2008) suggests that some viruses can damage the central nervous system, and this can lead to autism. She further states that complications during pregnancy and contact with viruses such as rubella could lead to autism in some cases. One of the recent theories about vaccinations was started by Wakefield et al.'s (1998) paper, which reported MMR vaccine as a possible cause of autism. However, most of the authors have since withdrawn their support for this theory. Recent research evidence (MRC 2001; Honda et al. 2005) also proves that MMR vaccine is not a cause of autism.

As can be seen from the above discussion, autism is a complex condition where a number of new developments are taking place.

However, there is no clear evidence which suggests the exact cause of autism in all cases. The unclear nature of the causation makes it especially difficult for some family members to accept the condition and it is important that you, as a professional, are able to listen to their concerns and guide them towards the appropriate support services.

Summary of the main points

- Autism spectrum is a broad label used to describe children who have difficulties in social communication and flexible thinking.
- The way autism affects each individual can vary. The word 'spectrum' is used to denote this disparity in the presentation of the condition.
- Autism is one of the most common disabilities, with the current figures suggesting about 1 per cent of the population are affected by the condition.
- The exact cause of autism is still unknown, although the research suggests biological causes based on genetic links and abnormality in brain development.

Activity time

- Before you move on to the next chapter, revisit the case studies of Ben and Mohamud in this chapter. Try to identify which of their behaviours will qualify them for a diagnosis of autism spectrum.
- If you have access to an early years setting, observe a child diagnosed with autism in your setting. Make a note of their behaviours and compare how these are different to a child without autism. Try and classify the identified behaviours under the two areas of social communication and flexible thinking. If you can, observe another child with autism and classify their behaviours as well. Compare how similar or different are the two children on the autism spectrum.

CHAPTER

2

Identifying and getting a diagnosis

As an early years practitioner it is likely that you are one of the first professionals who come into contact with the child and their family. It is also likely that on the basis of your knowledge of child development you are able to notice differences in the child and may want to talk to the family about them. Alternatively, the family may seek your advice if they are concerned about the child's behaviour or progress. This chapter aims to provide more details about some of the characteristics of autism which can alert you to the possibility of a child having the condition. It also provides an understanding of the diagnostic procedure generally followed and how you can support the family and the child throughout this process.

Unlike some other disabilities, autism is not diagnosed on the basis of a medical examination but on observation of certain behaviours. A trained professional will need to observe these behaviours to reach a diagnosis and to rule out any other conditions. There are some formal screening tools which can be used by professionals such as health visitors. The Checklist for Autism in Toddlers (CHAT) was one screening tool developed to identify the possibility of autism in children at the age of 18 months. CHAT has nine questions, covering the main areas of difficulties, which need to be answered by parents, and some additional items for the professionals to answer. However, the reliability of this tool is not 100 per cent. Baron-Cohen et al. (1996) conducted a follow-up study of the children with whom CHAT was used. They found that a majority of children identified as being at risk following the CHAT did receive a diagnosis of autism. But there were also a number of other children CHAT did not identify as being at risk who were diagnosed as being on the autism spectrum in later years. This highlighted that a screening tool such as CHAT, although useful to a certain extent, cannot be used as the sole method of identification.

The Autism Research Centre team at Cambridge have since developed an updated screening tool called Quantitative Checklist for Autism in Toddlers (Q-CHAT), which is available on their website. Similarly, Robins et al. (1999) have modified the original CHAT as the M-CHAT, which can also be found online. A latest study by Nygren et al. (2012) used M-CHAT along with observations and has found that this combination can provide a more reliable indication of autism – highlighting that even these modified versions cannot be accurate on their own. Currently, some other screening tools to identify autism in children as young as 1 year are also being developed. As an early years practitioner you may or may not have access to all these screening tools. However, you are one of the professionals who observe the child for long periods and in different settings. Therefore, having some basic understanding of the core features can enable you to help the child and his family. The following list provides some of the key features. If you see a combination of the following behaviours it is possible that the child may be on the autism spectrum.

Social-communication skills

The child may not point at objects or people for communicative purposes.

The child may not follow your eye gaze or pointing gesture.

The child uses eye contact inappropriately (not looking at all, or staring continuously).

There is limited use of facial expressions or social smiling.

The child may not have any speech or has 'lost' their speech.

Where speech is prevalent, the child repeats words or phrases and does not use them for communication.

The use of intonation or accent is unusual (for example, a child uses an American accent when they have no connection with the USA).

The child uses other people's hands or body as a tool when they want something.

The child may take language literally.

The child finds it difficult to share interests and objects with others, or does not share at all.

The child finds it difficult to take turns with more than one person in a game or conversation.

The child displays difficulty in playing with other children.

The child does not respond to their name.

The child seems to find it difficult to understand social rules and customs.

Conversely, the child may insist on following the same set of rules, with no flexibility.

The child loses interest in conversations which are not related to their favourite topic.

The child does not seek comfort from others when they are in pain or distress.

The child shows inappropriate emotional responses to people's actions.

Imagination and odd behaviour

The child displays unusual repetitive behaviours (such as flapping hands, rocking, and spinning objects).

The child walks on his tiptoes.

The child may not use toys in a conventional way.

The child may not get involved in pretend or imaginary play, or follows similar story sequences every time.

The child finds it difficult to cope with any changes to routine (such as staff changes or activity changes).

The child develops his own routines and rituals, and insists on following them.

The child may show self-injurious behaviour such as biting or hitting himself.

The child responds in an unusual way to sounds, sights, textures and tastes (for example, sniffs people, covers his ears when music is played, won't play with wet sand).

Sharing your doubts

If, following your observations, you feel that a child could be on the autism spectrum, be careful about how you approach his or her family with this information. As highlighted above, screening tools are not always reliable, and your suspicion could be a false alarm. It is always advisable to have a meeting with the family to share some of your observations. Allocate time and space for this meeting, as family members can get distressed and may need privacy. Try not to state that you think their child has autism, but engage with the family in a discussion to find out if they have observed some of the behaviours you have noticed in the early years setting. It is possible that children with autism may show different behaviours in the home setting compared to an early years setting, where they have to interact with other children and adults. Therefore, if the family state that they have never observed the behaviours you have indicated, invite them into the setting to observe the child or to record an activity. If the family do share your concerns, suggest to them what they can do next to get a clear diagnosis of their child's condition.

Diagnostic process and tools

Once a referral has been made, a specialist paediatrician will usually invite the child and his family for a multidisciplinary team appointment. The appointment generally tends to take about two to three hours, but can be longer or shorter depending on the way different services are structured. The team can include professionals such as speech therapists, psychologists, health visitors and educational professionals. During this appointment the professionals may ask the family a range of questions as well as engaging the child in some activities. Although these activities can look like nothing more than play, the diagnostic teams use these games to identify the areas of difficulties and strengths. The most common diagnostic tools which are used during these appointments in the UK are the Autism Diagnostic Interview and the Autism Diagnostic Observation Schedule.

The Autism Diagnostic Interview – Revised (ADI-R) (Rutter et al. 2005) is an interview-based diagnostic tool, where a structured interview is used to gather information from the family in all the areas that children on the autism spectrum find difficult. The questions are open-ended, reducing the chances of family members providing biased information, and the scoring gathered helps in providing a diagnosis on the basis of DSM-IV or ICD-10. The Autism Diagnostic

Observation Schedule (ADOS) (Lord et al. 2003) is an observational tool that the professionals use while engaging the child in a range of activities. They will be looking for the symptoms of autism spectrum while the child is involved in the activities. The child's performance in each of these activities is scored, which leads to a diagnosis.

Sometimes professionals may use other observation- or interview-based tools for the purpose of diagnosis. The Diagnostic Interview for Social and Communication Disorders (DISCO) is one such interview-based diagnostic tool. It covers the whole autism spectrum and provides information about additional conditions such as attention deficit disorder, Tourette's syndrome and obsessive compulsive disorder (Wing et al. 2002). Its use is still limited to certain centres in the UK. Various diagnostic tools that are used to assess cognitive, language and social skills can be used in conjunction with the autism-specific assessments.

Differential diagnosis

Following the diagnostic appointment it is likely that the professionals may give a range of labels to explain the child's condition. Professionals increasingly use the term autism spectrum disorder or pervasive developmental disorders (PDD) as a generic diagnostic label to describe anyone on the autism spectrum. However, some may use other specific terms such as autism, Asperger syndrome, atypical autism, and pervasive developmental disorder – not otherwise specified (PDD-NOS). These labels are explained here to enable you to support the family and the child.

Autism and Asperger syndrome are considered to be more or less the same condition, falling on the different ends of the continuum. The main difference between the two according to ICD-10 and DSM-IV is that in Asperger syndrome the areas of speech development and cognitive skills are not affected before the age of three. There are also suggestions that motor skills (gross and fine) are affected in children with Asperger syndrome, which is not so in children with autism. As explained in the previous chapter, the new DSM-V is proposing that Asperger syndrome as a separate category is dropped because of the limited evidence that it is a clinically distinct category. Even if the label is being used it is highly unlikely that this term will be applied to young children. Professionals are more likely to use the term high-functioning autism to explain that the child does not have significant learning difficulties. PDD-NOS or atypical autism is a diagnosis which is used when the child does not show all the features of autism, or the age of onset is later than 36 months.

Some other terms you may hear in relation to autism are Rett's syndrome, childhood disintegrative disorder and pathological demand avoidance (PDA). Rett's and childhood disintegrative disorder were part of the DSM-IV criteria for pervasive developmental disorders (PDD). But since the prognosis of Rett's is very different to autism, this book does not cover this. The characteristics shown by children with childhood disintegrative disorder can be very similar to those of autism, other than that the child appears to regress after developing normally for some time. Although professionals in the UK are increasingly classifying PDA as part of the autism spectrum, this has not been agreed internationally yet, and therefore this is also not covered by this book.

Role of family and early years practitioners in diagnosis

The role of family is integral to getting an appropriate diagnosis. Howlin (2000) suggests that if a family have a good experience during the diagnostic process they are more likely to have a positive attitude towards the diagnostic label. Although early years professionals are generally not part of the diagnostic team, you can try to make the experience positive by helping the family during the process. Clinical diagnosis is generally conducted in an artificial environment which is different from the child's regular environment. Children may behave differently in such settings and their performance may not mirror their actual potential or behaviour. I have known children who were intimidated by the scenario and hence were wrongly diagnosed with autism. Similarly, there were also children who performed very well due to the structure that was provided in the assessment, thus being denied an appropriate diagnosis. Although some professionals assess/observe the child in the natural environment as well, time constraints mean this is a rare occurrence. It is important that you, along with the family, help the child to be prepared for the change in routine. Most children with autism find it difficult to cope in new situations and with new people if they are not aware of the changes. Use visuals (such as pictures, photographs or line drawings) to explain about the changes in the routine and what may happen at the appointment. If you are able to show the child photographs beforehand of the professionals involved in the assessment process, this may reduce the possibility of distress at the appointment.

Along with the child you also need to help the parents in their preparation. No one knows the child as well as the parents do. Therefore, parents and family members play a major role in providing appropriate information in such situations. As an early years practitioner you can encourage the family to collect all the data that they feel is relevant before the assessment and write it up. Formal meetings can be intimidating at times and having a written report will ensure that the parents have expressed all their concerns. If possible, provide a broad idea to the family about the kind of information that would be relevant for the diagnosis. Take care not to provide any leading questions. If possible, send a detailed report about the child's performance in the early years setting. This will help the professionals involved in the diagnosis to have a broader and more accurate view about the child's functioning level. It is also a good idea to suggest to the family that they take someone along with them to the appointment so that this person can concentrate on the information being given and raise any pre-agreed questions. Sometimes families can find it distressing when their child is diagnosed with autism and may not be able to take in all the information that is provided by the professionals, and having an additional person can help in revisiting the information at a later stage. Also encourage the family to request a follow-up appointment with the professionals when they can go back with any further questions they may have.

Reactions to the diagnosis

Not so long ago it was considered that all families who have a child with disabilities go through different stages such as shock, denial, sadness and anger before they move towards adaptation to the new reality and accept their child's diagnosis (Drotar et al. 1975). Although it is true that some families could go through various stages of reaction, these are not necessarily developmental in nature. Families could miss some of these stages before they move on to the next stage or could revisit similar emotions at various points in their lives. How a family reacts to the diagnosis is based on their own individual circumstances and experiences. For example, Nissenbaum et al. (2002) have found that the initial shock was less likely where the family already suspected the condition. Such families may in fact feel a sense of relief if they had suspected that something was abnormal with their child for a long time. Some families could see getting a diagnosis as a route to accessing a range of services and support for their child and themselves.

Family reactions could also depend on their own understanding of autism and how the information has been shared with them. For example, professionals often use technical jargon, making an assumption that families will understand these terms – which may not always be the case. I know of a mother who was not worried after receiving her son's diagnosis and expected that the child would become 'normal' because she understood the term developmental disabilities to mean that the disabilities go away as the child grows up. Therefore it is important that you spend some time with the family to ensure that they have understood the information appropriately.

The perceptions of people around us influence our own attitudes and beliefs to a certain extent, and one of the main worries for parents at the point of diagnosis is how to share the information with other family members and friends (Nissenbaum et al. 2002). If it is possible, perhaps you could suggest having a meeting with some of the immediate family to help the parents share the diagnosis, or alternatively signpost them to local support groups who may provide information about sharing the news. Different communities can have different perceptions of disability (Perepa 2007), and it is necessary that you have some understanding of how the family perceives disability or autism to support them appropriately. Have a meeting with the family to get an insight into their own concepts of autism and disability.

Another aspect that a number of parents and families want to know about at this stage is how their child with autism will progress. This is a rather difficult question to answer as there is very little research which has looked at this issue. One of the few studies to be conducted was by Howlin et al. (2004), who found that the prognosis of individuals without any additional learning difficulties was better in their adulthood compared to those who had learning difficulties. However, autism is full of exceptions and it would be wiser not to provide a judgement of the child's future abilities and to explain to the family that all children with autism do make progress and are capable of learning.

What if a diagnosis is not given?

It is possible that, in spite of your judgement and the family's feelings, some children may not receive a diagnosis of autism or any other disability at the point of assessment. If this happens to be the case with the family you are working with, find out why the professionals decided that the child does not have autism or any other disability. As mentioned earlier, some children perform extremely well in a well-structured environment. You and the family may suggest that the professionals visit the early years setting or the family home to see the child in a less structured setting where the child is expected to interact with their peers.

Similarly, some families may find the assessment situation particularly stressful and may not share all their concerns or underplay them with the fear of being judged. Research has found that getting a diagnosis can be particularly difficult for families who belong to lower socio-economic groups (Goin-Kochel et al. 2006). This is the reason why preparing the family can help them. Of course, it is just as likely that both your concerns are false alarms, and if that is the case you may want to monitor the child for a few more months and then seek another referral if required.

Summary of the main points

- Certain characteristics can be used to identify the possibility of autism; however, a formal diagnosis by trained professionals is required to rule out any other possible conditions.
- Share your doubts with the family in a sensitive way and signpost them to appropriate referral services.
- Prepare the family and the child for the diagnostic appointment.
- Provide support to the family after the appointment, whether or not the child gets the diagnosis of autism.
- Remember that each family's reaction to getting a diagnosis can be different and that it is important to understand their perceptions of the situation.

Activity time

- Find out what is the referral process in your local area for getting a diagnosis of autism.
- Read the following statements and consider how you would respond to the family if you were working with them. Consider also what your reactions reveal about your own perceptions about autism (activity based on the exercise by Dale (1996)).
  - My child cannot be autistic. I have never committed any sins to deserve a child with disabilities.
  - I am so relieved to have finally got a diagnosis for my child. I always knew that there was something different about her.
  - All they did at the assessment was to ask my grandchild to play with a few things. There was no proper test. How can they say he has autism? I don't believe their diagnosis.
  - I cannot see any point in my life. I always wanted a perfect child and now I have one with disabilities.
  - If only the doctors had provided adequate care at the time of delivery, my child would never have been disabled.

Useful websites

Early support information for parents: www.education.gov.uk/publications/standard/publicationDetail/Page1/ES12

Information about autism in other languages: www.autism.org.uk/about-autism/in-other-languages.aspx

3

Working with families

Receiving a diagnosis of autism can change the dynamics of that child's family. There is an increasing interest in understanding what the impact of autism on family life can be. Most of this tends to focus on parents, and has recently started to be extended to siblings. Looking at the majority of the research in the field it appears that the definition of 'family' is still considered to be two-parent families with siblings; however, as we are aware, this is not always the case. Families can come in all kinds of combinations and shapes including single parents, same-sex parents, step-parents, adoptive parents, extended family members. Therefore, the first step in working with families is to understand the individual structure of that family. The specific issues and impact on each family will be different and will need to be understood on an individual basis. This chapter attempts to provide information about some of the salient topics raised in research and gives some pointers to consider while working in partnership with families. I would like to highlight here that, while this chapter primarily focuses on the impact on the family of having a child with autism, not all the issues that a family faces will be related to autism: it is important to remember that there may be family dynamics in play outside of the child's autism.

Impact of autism on the family

The emotional impact of having a child with autism can be on two levels, one which is led by personal feelings and one that is generated by interaction with others. Some parents could be blaming themselves for their child's autism. This can be based on their understanding that autism is genetic and hence they may have passed on the 'defective' genes. Or they may blame themselves for giving vaccinations such as MMR because of the media attention on this as a possible cause of autism. Some families may consider themselves to be guilty because of some sin they have committed. Parents whose children appeared to progress normally and then lost their abilities may also blame themselves for doing something wrong. If parents are facing such feelings, they will need some reassurance and opportunity to express their fears. However, in your attempt to reassure do not underemphasize the genetic cause of autism, especially if the parents are thinking of having another child and seek your opinion about the likelihood of the next child having autism. In such situations, it would be best to refer the parents to genetic counselling to get a professional view on the possibility of this happening, as families with one child with autism can have another child on the spectrum.

At times, the diagnosis of autism can de-skill the parents and they may stop trusting their instincts, especially when the child with autism is not reciprocating the parents' interactions. While some parents may need specific support with particular issues, they must be encouraged to have faith in their own judgements; otherwise there is a risk that they will become overdependent on expert support (Whitaker 2002).

Some researchers have found that, because family life tends to be focused on the child with autism and gets restricted because of the rules and routines of the child, parents feel that it lacks a sense of 'normality' (Woodgate et al. 2008). Therefore, while you are providing strategies for the child, do not miss the bigger picture of the whole family and the effect your ideas may have on their time and resources. Parents may experience feelings of sadness, jealousy and anger when they are in social situations with typically developing children as such situations highlight the limitations of their own children (Woodgate et al. 2008). These feelings can recur at different points of life, and some parents may choose to reduce their interactions with other families because of this. You need to be sensitive about this when asking families to visit the early years setting, and allocate some time to talk to the family members if need be.

Withdrawing from society, of course, can lead to isolation, especially if they are single parents or have very few social contacts, such as newly immigrated families (Woodgate et al. 2008), as there are fewer sources of support for the parents. As discussed in the previous chapter, the way individuals within a family react to the diagnosis of autism varies, and this can influence their own attitudes to their lives. As each member of the family is taking a different path in understanding and accepting the diagnosis, it is possible that in some families there are disparities in how both the partners (in two-parent families) and the extended family approach the subject. For example, Gray (2003) found that the way mothers and fathers cope with a diagnosis is different, with mothers engaged in talking about the emotional impact while fathers tend to focus more on their work. This can leave some members within the family feeling more isolated at times (Woodgate et al. 2008) as they may not always be able to reach out to each other.

It has been reported that parents of children with autism experience higher levels of stress than parents of typically developing children (Brobst et al. 2009) or children with other disabilities (Abbeduto et al. 2004). Different researchers have attributed this higher level of stress to a range of possible causes. One opinion states that it is the result of the negative behaviours exhibited by the child with autism rather than the severity of their autism (Estes et al. 2009). Parents have also identified other causes for the stress, such as worry about their child's future, not finding time to spend with their partner and other members of the family, financial strain experienced by them because of one of them giving up their job (Cassidy et al. 2008). It is not unusual that families may have to make changes in their work patterns and career goals, with some parents completely giving up work to look after their child on the autism spectrum. This is more likely where the family has more than one child on the autism spectrum or with other disabilities.

It is usually the mothers whose career is affected by their child's autism. Perhaps this is one of the reasons why it has also been suggested that the level of stress experienced by fathers and mothers could be different. There seems to be variation in which characteristics of the child cause stress in mothers and fathers. Hastings et al. (2005) found that while mothers were usually concerned about the autism features of their child and their disability per se, fathers were more worried about the maladaptive behaviours shown by their child with autism. This shows us that the reactions to, and therefore the impact of, autism can vary considerably from one family member to another.

As stated earlier, some of the reasons could relate to interaction with the community. For instance, in the research conducted by Woodgate et al. (2008) it was found that some parents felt isolated because society did not understand their child's autism. This is a common statement that many parents have mentioned to me over the years. A child with autism does not necessarily appear to have a disability and it is easy for strangers to consider that the child is being badly brought up and naughty. A mother once narrated to me her experience of taking her son swimming, where a complete stranger came up to her and said that the reason her son was not behaving in the pool was because she could not control him and that, in addition, she appeared to be a single mother! Such comments can not only cause distress but can contribute to further isolation. Another cause of stress could be trying to find appropriate educational placements and interventions for their child with autism (Gray 2003) and fighting for appropriate resources. In addition, some parents commented that the main reason for their stress was getting the professionals to accept their child's needs and strengths (Hodge and Runswick-Cole 2008). This puts the onus on you as a professional to relieve the stress being experienced by the family by listening to them and understanding their concerns, and helping them to access the required services.

Impact on siblings

Andrew is working on a model that he needs to take to his school. As he goes down to bring some newspaper Sarah, his sister who has autism, walks into his room and starts pulling the model apart. Andrew is aghast when he sees what happened to his model. It is times like these when he wishes that his sister did not have autism. He also feels guilty for wanting to hurt her, even though he knows that she did not mean to spoil his work.

Research on the experiences of siblings is limited and the existing information provides an uneven picture. Petalas et al. (2009) found that siblings of children with autism are at greater risk of emotional and behavioural problems. This view is also shared by Fisman et al. (2000), who argue that the brothers and sisters of children with autism are likely to experience psychological maladjustment, poor self-concept and impaired social competence. This may be because some siblings consider themselves to be invisible in their family context as a lot of attention is given to the child on the autism spectrum; some others feel that they need to compensate for their sibling with autism by being good at everything (Safer 2002). However, other researchers disagree that siblings of children with autism show any significant differences in psychological adjustment compared to siblings of typically developing children (Verté et al. 2003; Hastings 2006). Yet others state that these siblings actually show higher levels of social competence and positive behaviour adjustment (Kaminsky and Dewey 2002; Macks and Reeve 2006). In fact a number of professionals in the field of special education that I know have siblings with autism or other special needs, which supports the view expressed above. Not all people who have a sibling with autism develop as a consequence a negative attitude towards their brother or sister, or towards life in general. This mixed picture also highlights the individual nature of family experiences and shows that generalizations should not be made purely on the basis of information gathered from other sources. Nevertheless, when considering providing support to families, siblings' needs should also be considered; after all, autism is part of their life from childhood and beyond.

There are a few organizations which have started providing siblings workshops and activities. Even if you are unable to provide such activities within your own setting, it would be worth sharing information with the family about local organizations which do. Siblings often want to understand their brother or sister's condition. There is an increasing number of books available aimed at providing such information to the siblings. Siblings may also want to spend time with their parents when they can be the centre of attention. Information about befriending projects, short-break schemes and play clubs can help the parents to send their child with autism to a different activity with trained professionals while they spend quality time with their other children. Parents may also need to think of practical ideas such as providing the sibling with a lockable box where they can store their precious things or, for situations such as Andrew's, even having a lock on the door.

Positive influences

Most of the research on the impact of autism on families tends to focus on the negative influences only. However, not all families experience such negativity, and some have said that having someone with autism in their family has helped to unify them and encouraged them to develop more patience (Bayat 2007). This is certainly true from my experience as I have seen a number of such families which do enjoy normal life. Many autism charities across the world have been formed by parents who wanted to share their knowledge, raise awareness about autism and set up appropriate services. Woodgate et al. (2008) found that parents developed a positive attitude by celebrating the differences and learning to accept their child's characteristics. Bayat (2007) suggests that families which are flexible and have good communication between them are more likely to have a positive attitude towards having a family member with autism. Bayat adds that it is important for the families and professionals to focus on the strengths of the individual with autism to develop this positive attitude. Therefore, it is necessary that in your interactions with the family you not only focus on the needs of the child but also discuss his strengths.

Another main factor which can help the family to have a positive approach to life is having adequate sources of support. It has been suggested that families which have informal sources of support (such as from their partners, family and friends) are less likely to feel stressed and tend to have a positive attitude to life (Cassidy et al. 2008; Ekas et al. 2010). While some families have access to such support, this may not always be the case when families live far away from the rest of their relatives – as can be the case, for example, with families from minority ethnic communities. Therefore more formal sources of support may be required. Hall and Graff (2010) report that parental support groups and access to information can also contribute to reducing family stress levels. Therefore providing families with information about workshops or parent training programmes such as the National Autistic Society's EarlyBird or Help programmes in the UK, or Hanen, or portage programmes can be beneficial. These parent programmes can often lead to other sources of support for the parents by interacting with other parents who have children on the autism spectrum. Not all families may want to come for formal support group meetings and may even find them a bit daunting. Lock et al. (2010) suggest that having more informal ways of meeting, such as running family fun days which are open to all the family members and have relevant activities for them, can provide support to more families. They have also found that such activities attract parents who often do not attend support group meetings and families from minority ethnic groups.

Working in partnership

Families are one of the biggest resources that all of us have throughout our lives. This is also the case for children with autism, for whom their family members could be the most constant sources of support and help, unlike paid professionals who may change at various points. Acknowledging this source and working in partnership with the family is essential to ensure the progress of children with autism, at home and in the educational setting (Mesibov et al. 2004; Charman et al. 2011), as they may have difficulties in generalizing skills from one setting to another. Marshall and Mirenda (2002) comment that effective parent–professional collaboration not only helps the professionals acquire a better insight into the family situation but can also help the parents to be more accepting of each other's parenting styles. Although the term 'partnership working' is often used in literature and policies, its meaning is generally not clearly explained. Is partnership limited to using parents and other family members as informants, or do we actually mean equal partnership where family members have an equal voice and say in what is being decided for them?

Dale (1996), in her book, provides five different models of partnership: expert model, co-teacher model, parent as a consumer, empowerment model and negotiating model, which I will briefly describe here.

Expert model: In the expert model the professional is the fountain of all knowledge and judgements are made by the professionals with little consultation with the family. The role of family members is primarily restricted to providing information when they are asked to.

Co-teacher model: Here the parent is considered as a resource who will be able to help in delivering the intervention for the child, which is developed by the professionals. Parents then give feedback about the issues in implementing the programme to the professional, who accordingly provides further guidance.

Parent as consumer: With the role of a consumer, the parent considers which services are appropriate for their child and buys into them accordingly. The professionals have a role to provide the services as experts, but also help the parents in making decisions by giving them information about their options. This means that the professional will need to have a good understanding of the family's needs and aims. Parents in this model are considered to have expert knowledge of their child and the ability to make appropriate decisions.

Empowerment model: This recognizes that each family has particular needs and that parents may be at different stages in their readiness for partnership working. The professionals need to understand these differences and empower the parents to become effective partners. Parents still need to be part of all decisions, and the power of decision-making lies with them as in the parent as consumer model.

Negotiating model: This acknowledges that parents and professionals both have important contributions to make but they may have different functions. Decisions are therefore made mutually after negotiation. Although the professional may still have the expert knowledge of the subject, parents are considered to have their own expertise with their child.

As can be seen, each of these models defines partnership in a different way. I think all of these models can be used at various points according to the needs of the family. What is important for a partnership is mutual involvement and agreed roles and responsibilities where both parties are clear about what their contribution will be. They also need to have a desire to work in collaboration and share their responsibilities, achieving agreed goals. This would require a certain level of honesty and information sharing between the partners and sensitivity to each other's needs.

Issues in maintaining a partnership

Working in a partnership is not always easy for either of the parties. It is likely that the family's beliefs about the cause of autism could be different from yours; therefore they may want to pursue a different course of action to the one you are comfortable with. For example, a family may strongly believe that their child's autism is a result of sins committed in a previous life and that penitence is the only way to overcome their autism – which may not be your idea of the causes of autism or the approach for intervention. Differences have been observed in how professionals and parents view the impact of autism on the family (Dillenburger et al. 2010). Therefore, the interventions programme and the support that the professionals offer may not be appropriate for the family.

Differences can occur over interventions even if you agree on the causes. For example, there may be general agreement that sensory issues are a major need for the child, but the family may want to try auditory integration therapy while you may not believe in it. Or you may want to use pictures as a means of communication but the parents may feel it will hinder their child's speech development. Families could also have different expectations from you as a professional. For instance, when I tried to negotiate the best course of action for one child with autism, his family was baffled as to why I was asking their opinion. They thought that perhaps I was new to the field and said they would like to see someone senior!

The last reason which can hamper collaborative working is your own attitudes towards parents. Sometimes families get labelled as being difficult, demanding or paranoid by the professionals, and when these views are shared by colleagues it can colour your interactions with the family. It has been reported that sometimes parents follow the opinions of the professionals even if they do not agree with them, simply to avoid being labelled (Hodge and Runswick-Cole 2008).

Basis of a successful partnership

So, how can a successful partnership be maintained with all these difficulties? I think the main thing to start with is having clarity about everyone's roles and boundaries. You may have to revisit these on more than one occasion to ensure that they are absolutely clear for everyone. Effective partnership working also requires having some empathy and understanding of the family's perception of the situation. It is very tempting to think that we as professionals know how a family may experience an issue, based on our own previous knowledge, but remember that each family is made up of a different set of individuals and you need to understand their own experiences without making any preconceived judgements. This will also help you to understand what the family considers to be their needs and will enable you to provide appropriate support. It is important that the strategies you provide fit into the family belief system and meet their concerns. Parents appreciate it when professionals listen to them and see their child as an individual rather than a label (Hodge and Runswick-Cole 2008). You also need to be flexible in your approach and willing to change the partnership model on the basis of the family's needs. For example, when the family is looking for a primary school for their child and have no experience of the education system in the country they may want to go back to you being the expert for a while.

The strength of a partnership is also based on how you communicate with the family. Use open-ended questions to help them take control of the conversation and to express their needs, and listen to what they are saying. In your conversations try to keep the information simple and avoid using jargon. Because of the genetic nature of autism it is possible that some of the family members may also share certain features and may need a clearer way of communication. It is helpful if you structure the information and explain to them how you will be providing information. For example, 'In this meeting we will be discussing three things. First, we will inform you how Tom is performing in the nursery. Then we will discuss how you think he is developing. Finally, we will decide which areas to focus on for the next three months.' Whenever you are having a meeting it is always a good idea to provide the information at least a day before the meeting so that the family is well prepared. Similarly, give the key points of the discussion to the family as soon as possible afterwards, in a format that the parents can refer back to; ask the family which format will be most useful for them rather than making assumptions. For example, some families from minority ethnic communities may not be able to read their community language and prefer information in English as some of their extended family members will be able to read it for them. While working with families from minority ethnic communities avoid using family members as interpreters and use professional interpreters. Sometimes members of the family may not share the information you pass on with the others for various reasons, and having your own interpreter will avoid such situations.

Partnership working is ongoing work and needs regular thought given to it. Children on the autism spectrum often will not be able to tell their families what they have been doing and families are dependent on the information they will get from you. Therefore, think of how you will share the information. Home–school books can be one possible way, but other means such as emails, text messages or home visits can also be used. In your communication, be realistic and try to avoid giving too positive or too negative impressions. Sometimes early years settings only use home–school books when the child has done something wrong and so families avoid using these as a means of communication. It is important that effective ways of communication are always maintained to nurture a good working relationship with the family.

Summary of the main points

- The impact of autism can be different on each family and on different members of the family.
- It is important that you understand individual families' needs and provide support in the most appropriate way.
- Although partnership working can be challenging, it is important to invest in developing this. Effective means of communication plays an important role in developing good working relationships.

Activity time

- Think about particular events and activities in your life that you enjoy doing with your family and friends. How might someone with autism experience these and what could be the implications of this on family life?
- Think about your interactions and relationships with your doctor, your line manager, and a close friend. Which models of partnership does each of these relationships involve? Thinking about your work with families, which style of interaction do you usually follow and why? Consider alternative approaches you can take. (Adapted from Dale's (1996) activity.)
- Read the following case study and consider what the issues are here from the professional's perspective.

    Imran is a bright little boy. I have tried working with his parents. His parents seem to agree with all the strategies that I suggest, but nothing is followed. His mother helps him with all his daily living tasks, not allowing him to develop his independence. When Imran makes any 'mistakes' his father would get annoyed and would shout at him – which does not help Imran's self-confidence either. His father does not pay attention to any of the suggestions that I am providing. In fact he is often not there when I make my home visits.

    What are the things that are making the professional uncomfortable here, and why? How could she or he work with this family?

    Now think of a situation with a family when you had difficulties in establishing a working relationship. What were the things that you were uncomfortable about in the relationship and why was this? Looking back, what could you have done to make it work?

Useful websites

Autism Education Trust toolkit for working with families: www.autismeducationtrust.org.uk/resources/toolkits.aspx

The National Autistic Society: www.autism.org.uk

Contact a Family: www.cafamily.org.uk

Sibs: www.sibs.org.uk

4

Social interaction

Kanner (1943) identified social difficulties as a core feature of autism. The choice of the label 'autism' itself is based on this idea that people with autism are happy to be within themselves. While this may be true for some children, others may want to interact with people. In fact, Wing (1996) describes four types of social behaviour observed in people on the spectrum: aloof, passive, active but odd, and the overly formal group. It is children who are considered part of the aloof group that are mostly associated with having autism. According to Wing (1996), children who are passive accept social interactions but do not actively seek any interaction, whereas children in the third group try to initiate interactions but these are not always appropriate. The fourth group are like 'little professors', and are extremely polite and formal and follow all social rules very strictly. Children in all these categories may try to interact with others but may withdraw if their attempts fail. This is the main reason that social interaction skills need to be developed in children on the spectrum so that they can choose whether and when they want to interact with others.

Adam was playing with his dinosaur in the play corner. Sally wanted to play with Adam and asked him if she could join in. Adam handed her the toy but did not interact with her and sat in the corner. Sandra, one of the staff members, noticed this and suggested that perhaps he could choose something else. Adam got up and started running around the nursery.

Sandra remembered that she should give limited choices to Adam, and went back and suggested that he could go on the swing or to the sand tray. Adam repeated 'swing' and ran outside to the swing.

There is a lot of overlap between social and communication skills, as a number of initial social interactions lead to the development of communication skills. However, I am attempting to differentiate these on the basis of the diagnostic criteria discussed in Chapter 2. To provide a quick reminder, the main areas that are considered to be difficult for children with autism are: using socially appropriate eye contact, facial expressions and body language; engaging in joint attention or spontaneous sharing of interests with others; developing peer relationships; understanding other people's emotions; understanding social rules; and modulating their behaviour accordingly. Some of these differences can be noticed in the case study above where Adam did not share his toys with Sally, nor did he seek someone's attention to request for help. As the above list shows, these skills and behaviours are not easy to teach and can take a long time. This in turn can make them age-inappropriate, and this must be borne in mind while teaching specific skills. It may be more beneficial in the long run to teach the underlying social expectations and rules. Before we go ahead we will look at what makes social interaction so difficult for children on the autism spectrum.

Theory of mind

This theory was initially suggested by Baron-Cohen et al. (1985) when they reported their 'Sally–Ann task' results. They found that children with autism did not realize that the information they have is not necessarily shared by others. It has been argued that this makes it difficult for people on the autism spectrum to empathize with others and understand how other people feel or think, and to predict what they might do in a particular situation or think about a topic. Various terms such as 'mind-blindness' or 'inability to mind-read' are also used to describe this concept.

Think of the number of times we use this ability to guess in our communication. For example, when you are at a party and your partner catches your eye and looks at the door. Once you have checked the door to see there is nothing of interest, you automatically understand that your partner is suggesting it is time to leave the party. In fact if you try watching a television drama without any sound it is likely that you will understand the main storyline because you can depend on your ability to understand others' intentions and anticipate outcomes. The theory of mind suggests that people with autism either have a delayed development of this ability or sometimes lack it altogether. This lack of knowledge makes social interaction unpredictable for children with autism as they may not understand the reasons for others' actions or anticipate the impact of their own actions on others.

Although this explanation is a possibility, there are also research-ers who have suggested that this theory cannot be used as an expla-nation for all people on the autism spectrum. In her study, Happe (1999) found that children with high-functioning autism or Asperger syndrome did not fail the tasks. Similarly, in research conducted by Yirmiya et al. (1998) children with developmental disabilities other than autism also showed difficulties in theory of mind tasks. Both studies suggested that the language ability of the person contributed towards the success of completing these tasks. Hobson (2002) queried whether the lack of theory of mind is a consequence of, rather than a reason for, the child's social inability. In spite of its limitations, this theory provides one possible explanation for the difficulties people on the autism spectrum have in social interactions.

Impaired interpersonal relatedness

According to Hobson (1993; 2002), from a very young age children show a preference for human beings and engage with them socially and emotionally. This happens because they come 'pre-wired' to respond to their carer's behaviour, which helps in developing emo-tional engagement with each other. This bond then helps the child to share the interests of the parents and leads to joint attention, where the child will follow the eye-gaze or pointing gesture of the carer. Hobson (2002) states that this shared attention helps the child in understanding that other people have mental states which could be similar to or different from his own, and can lead to joint attention and empathy. This understanding of others leads to awareness of the concept of self. Hobson, like Kanner (1943), argues that children with autism seem to lack the basic engagement with their carer, which then causes difficulties in developing a concept of other people, their mental states or the concept of their own individual self. Hobson (1993) provides the example of reversal of the pronouns 'I' and 'you' found in some children with autism as evidence to his point.

Jordan and Powell (1995) shared similar ideas about lack of sense of self in people on the spectrum. They state that the reason children with autism have difficulty in personal episodic memory is because they do not have a conscious awareness of what they are experiencing. They learn as if they are observing an activity rather than participating in it, which then makes them unable to take this knowledge to a new situation. However, this explanation does not provide a reason for the inability to develop a sense of self.

Developing attachment

Hobson's (1993) theory suggests that one way to help a child with autism in understanding emotions and developing empathy is re-establishing an attachment where the child understands the two-way nature of the relationship. Two different approaches, Son-Rise (or Options) and Intensive Interaction, following similar principles, attempt to address this area. The Options approach (Kaufman 1976) was devised by the Kaufmans to work with their own son who has autism, and later led to the opening of the Option Institute in the USA. Intensive Interaction (Nind and Hewett 1994) was developed as an approach for working with adults with learning disabilities. Although the finer details differ, the focus of both these approaches is on developing social and communication skills by establishing a relationship with the child. The emphasis is on spending time with the child and following his lead by imitating his actions. It is understood that by engaging with the child in this way and re-establishing the early interaction patterns, the child will gradually start performing an action to get a reaction from the adult. Once this starts happening, the adult could lead him to imitate their actions by expanding what the child does. This could be the first steps towards developing imitation, turn-taking skills and meaningful eye contact. Of course, for some children accepting shared physical space can itself be a challenge and a graded approach may be necessary. This could involve starting by sharing the same room but with ample physical space, before increasing the level of proximity.

> Jacob was sitting and playing with his blocks, putting them on top of each other. His key worker sat at a distance from him and copied Jacob's actions and the sounds he was making. Jacob noticed this and started making sounds and then looking at his key worker, who imitated them. After a few minutes of doing this his key worker knocked over his tower while saying 'boom'. Jacob gave him a startled look and then carried on. His key worker followed Jacob again and after a gap knocked over the tower again with the same sound. This time Jacob imitated him by knocking over his own tower.

The main criticism about these approaches is that they are labour-intensive. The Option Institute recommends parents to spend a number of hours one-to-one with their child in a distraction-free environment. Other than being a possible financial drain, there are also implications of the child missing opportunities to interact with his peers and lead a more 'normal' life. Intensive Interaction is less prescriptive about time and location. There is limited empirical research evidence for the efficacy of either of these approaches, but research using similar approaches (Wimpory et al. 2007) has seen an increase in the children's engagement.

Developing eye contact

Inappropriate use of eye contact is considered to be characteristic of autism and often draws the attention of others to the child if he either seems to be avoiding looking at others or stares at them. A number of people on the autism spectrum mention that this is because they find giving eye contact distressing and difficult. Some of them even say that they can either look or listen but not do both at the same time. Therefore the focus should be on developing eye contact when it is required for social interaction purposes. For example, you could stop singing the child's favourite song and wait to see if he will look at you as a request. If that happens, continue with the song. Even if the child does not look at you, start singing again after a few minutes' pause and do not force the child to look at you.

Joint attention means sharing your interest in an object or an event by looking at it, looking at the person you want to share it with, and then back again at the object. Most children develop this skill in early infancy. Children with autism tend to spot the object and then either pull the adult towards their desired object or make some other kind of indication, like crying, to show that they want the object, but they do not engage in joint attention. If the child you are working with is pulling you towards the object, you could try pulling back his hand and when he looks at you, look back at the desired object saying 'Oh, you want…'. This can slowly teach the child the stages of joint attention. As with everything, there will be exceptions and this might not work with all children. With some children you could join in their favourite activity and focus on what they are looking at or doing. A child will have to be ready to accept your company for this to happen. The idea is to help the child understand that sharing can be enjoyable. Storybooks or books that engage the child's interest could also be used for this. The adult could comment on the book, while making eye contact with the child and referring to the text or the pictures.

One other aspect that the child needs to learn while using eye contact for communication purposes is to ensure that the other person is also looking at him. In the Picture Exchange Communication System (PECS), which we will look at in more detail in the next chapter, the communicative partner actively avoids eye contact at one stage. When the child approaches the person with their picture card and taps the person to gain their attention, the communicative partner looks at the child and then responds to the request. Using this strategy could help the child to understand that the other person has to look at him to fulfil his wish.

Teaching emotions

Understanding emotions is complex as we not only depend on facial expressions but also body language, tone of voice and pitch to make sense of how someone is feeling. When teaching about emotions it is important that the child is exposed to these features for him to develop a good understanding. Most people start teaching emotions by using photographs to differentiate between them. There are also software packages such as Transporters and Mind-Reading (Baron-Cohen 2004) which can help with this kind of activity, as computers are often a good motivator for children with autism. If you are using photographs, use people from different ages, genders and ethnicities so that the child is able to associate the facial expressions of a variety of people. Start with two distinctive emotions such as happy and sad. Introduce the photo along with the name of the emotion. Focus on the facial aspects that represent that emotion – for instance, 'this lady is laughing so she is happy'. You could also imitate the expression.

Research has found that children with autism tend to focus around the mouth area of the face and hence may misinterpret an emotion. Ryan and Charragain (2010) found that rather than presenting a picture of the whole face, providing specific features and teaching the children to understand the emotions through them was more effective. This can be easily incorporated into an early years setting by developing some face puzzles or buying them. You can generalize their understanding by using cartoons or films. These will also help the child to focus on other aspects such as voice and body language and not just facial expressions. When the child is a bit older you could also role-play different scenarios or play games such as saying the same phrase with different emotions to enable him to differentiate between the tones.

However, if we take on board Jordan and Powell's (1995) view about children with autism lacking a sense of self, then awareness of his own feelings is important before the child is expected to have awareness of others' feelings. This would mean informing the child about his own emotional state, such as 'you are sad now' when you know that is how the child is feeling. This will slowly help the child to associate the label with how he is feeling, which can then lead to developing empathy for others' feelings. You could even draw his attention to how he looks when he feels a certain emotion, by showing him a mirror. You can also start drawing the child's attention to other people's emotions, including your own. Stories can be used for a similar purpose: you could pause at strategic points and ask the child how he thinks the character would be feeling. Remember that the child will need to be able to express this vocabulary and may need alternative means of communication such as symbols in some instances. Explaining to him what to do when someone is feeling a particular emotion or how he can express his own emotions comes only after this awareness is developed.

Explaining social rules

The unpredictability of social rules is one of the reasons that children with autism find social situations confusing. The TEACCH (Treatment and Education of Autistic and Related Communication Handicapped Children) programme believes that providing this information will reduce the anxiety. Where there are set rules – such as where to leave the coats in the setting, how many children are allowed at the water tray at a time – explain these rules visually, with pictures and written words. Remind the child before the activity by drawing his attention to the information. It is important for children with autism to know what is expected of them, so word your rules in a positive way. For example, rather than 'Do not push other children in the playground', say 'Wait for your turn' if that is what you mean. Visual clues about the expected rules in a new situation can also be provided when going on an outing so that the child knows what he needs to do. Do not be overzealous and give the child a long list of rules; provide only what he needs to know and what might resolve any confusion in the situation. As the child gets older it may also be important to start teaching which are absolute rules and non-negotiable, and which are flexible rules. For example, 'you should never put your finger in a plug socket' is a fixed rule, but we can sometimes eat our food while standing, such as at a party. It is necessary to involve families when deciding on these, as social rules are cultural in nature and it is likely that the norms for families will differ (Perepa 2008).

Social stories are another way to explain the expected behaviour in a situation. These were developed by Carol Gray (1995; 2000) and provide an insight into why a particular situation happens or what is expected in that setting. They are written for specific situations that the child is finding difficult and from his individual perspective; therefore it is important to keep the stories personalized. Gray (1995) suggested a specific format that needs to be followed while writing a social story and suggested using four kinds of sentences:

- descriptive sentences explain the main aspect of the situation
- perspective sentences share the internal state of the other people involved or the child's internal state
- directive sentences provide expected responses from the child with autism in the situations
- affirmative sentences confirm these as the expected common value or social norm.

Gray (2000) has later on added two other kinds of sentences: control sentences, which use analogies to explain situations; and cooperative sentences, which explain who can help the child in a given situation.

Although social stories are widely used with older children, I feel that they will need to be simplified to be used with young children or children with limited language comprehension, and this may not classify them as a social story as per Carol Gray's description. In one of the few studies that has evaluated the effectiveness of social stories in early years, Crozier and Tincani (2007) have found that although social stories were useful in reducing inappropriate behaviours and to an extent in encouraging new behaviours, some children needed additional prompts for them to be useful. They also found that not all children were able to maintain the improvement after the period of intervention. More research is needed to assess their applicability and effectiveness in early years settings.

Some other basic skills

There are often times in an early years setting when children need to wait – perhaps for their parent to come and pick them up, or for the story to finish before eating lunch. It is difficult for children to wait when they are unable to predict when their favourite activity will happen. It is useful if they understand the concept of waiting in a structured way where the children are motivated to engage in the activity but not too keen about having the object. You could encourage the child to pass on the object or toy to you and then ask him to 'wait' by using a hand gesture, or a symbol with written word (whatever you think will be appropriate). Give back the toy after a few seconds to begin with and then slowly increase the duration the child needs to wait for. It is important that you do this with a range of objects or toys of similar motivation level. Once the child is able to wait for a decent time, start using the same technique for more motivating objects or toys – but remember to bring down the time he needs to wait for it. It is also important that this approach is followed by different people in a range of situations for it to work effectively. Where waiting is for longer durations, using a visual timer such as an egg or sand timer will help the child to know how long he needs to wait. Where the wait is unpredictable, such as in a queue at the supermarket, a small card with counters to stick can be used to represent the time and these can be monitored on the basis of how quickly the line is progressing. When the card is full then you are ready to move on!

Another skill expected in an early years setting is to make choices. Children with autism can find the prospect of making choices from a range of things daunting and some may not make any, as in Adam's case study above. It is easier for someone like Adam if the choices are initially limited to two things. Once he is able to choose on a regular basis and understands what 'choice' means, the number of options can be increased. In the case of Adam, the nursery staff used only verbal instructions; some children may need pictorial representations to help them understand what is expected. Therefore, from the above scenario, pictures or symbols of swing and sand tray could have been shown.

> Salma is a verbal girl who likes to eat her lunch on a separate table, away from the other children. Today her mother gave her a new lunch box which she found difficult to open. Salma waited for some time, expecting her key worker to come and open the box for her. As the nursery was short of staff that day her key worker did not notice Salma. After waiting for some time Salma started thumping on the table; then a member of staff noticed the situation and opened her lunch box for her.

Because of the difficulties in theory of mind, children with autism may not always realize that they need to ask for help, and get frustrated that the other person is not helping them. It may be necessary to engineer situations where the child learns to request help. For example, give him his coat but do not offer to zip it. Encourage the child's peers to model asking for help. If the child is non-verbal, provide an alternative means of communication such as lifting up his hand, a symbol card, or even an iPad with the appropriate apps.

Reinforce the phrase while providing the child with the required support. As always, try this with different members of staff and family and create new situations to generalize the behaviour. If the child is able to understand, a social story can also be used.

Developing peer relationships

A number of social interactions are based on question/answer scenarios such as how someone is, or what they did over the weekend. Being able to answer such questions will help the child with autism to integrate with his peers and adults. During circle time sessions, use other children in the setting as the role models. Limit the number of peers you include to two or three, as children with autism tend to engage in more social initiations and interactions in small-group settings (Boyd et al. 2008). After the peers have modelled the appropriate response to the question, ask the child with autism the same question. Non-verbal children will again need an alternative means to communicate, as above. As the child gets more confident, start asking him the question first or randomly change the sequence in which you ask the questions.

With more able children it is important they are also able to express when they do not have the required information by saying something like 'I don't know'. You could introduce this in a similar structure to the above through play situations such as using a feely bag where you can ask the children whether they know what is inside the bag. Let the other children model the 'I don't know' response and then ask the child with autism. Later show him the object and then ask him what it is so that he does not start associating a negative answer with the activity. You can use a number of other situations to ask similar questions, such as what did I do yesterday evening, what did Sam have for breakfast, and so on.

Maintaining a social relationship needs some negotiation skills which children with autism will have to learn. Start with situations like choosing a game to play. Make a choice board with picture cards representing a favourite game of the child and another one that a peer or adult likes. Explain to the child that he has to choose which game to play, and that it is the other person's turn first. Let the other person choose the game that the child is not so keen on. Explain that once they finish the game that the other person has chosen, the child with autism will get a chance to choose his favourite game. Initially make sure that the first game does not last for very long. Then you could slowly extend the time period for the first game and reduce the time for his favourite game on some days, and the other way round on other days. Koegel et al. (2009) found that using social interactions along with rewards helped in developing social interaction skills in young children with autism. Expand situations where negotiation is required in the setting.

Due to their difficulties in social interactions, children with autism are more likely to experience rejection by their peers (Odom et al. 2006). Therefore, while working on developing specific social skills with children on the autism spectrum it is also important to raise awareness of the peers concerning accepting differences. Children are conscious of fairness and will challenge when they feel exceptions are being made. Be conscious of the terms you use to explain the differences. For example, if you say the child with autism is being naughty that will not help him to be accepted by his peers.

Setting up a buddy system may not only help the child with autism but will also raise the awareness of the other children in the setting. The buddy could help the child at unsupervised times by either explaining what is expected or being involved in social interactions with the child. It is advisable to have a small group of children (four to five) to act as buddies, with one or two children taking responsibility at any given time. Providing a small group rather than just one particular child will take care of situations when the buddy is absent. To motivate the other children a special badge or sticker can be given to say that they are the friend for the child with autism on that day, which makes it into a privilege. In research conducted by Kohler et al. (2007) they found that providing such rewards to the peers as well as giving them some training on how to interact with the child with autism can increase the number of social interactions. Try to keep the buddy responsibility for short bursts of time only.

It has been found that the frequency of social initiations and interactions increases when children are engaged in an activity that they or their peers have started (Boyd et al. 2008). This makes it vital that you have opportunities in your setting where structured child-initiated activities can take place. Having some kind of structure to the session where the children are expected to spend time in proximity to each other also seems to increase the number of initiations that a child with autism makes (Hauck et al. 1995; Bauminger et al. 2003; Reszka et al. 2012). This requires some careful planning for the layout of the setting as well as the timetable for the children. Book corners, snack times and computer times could be some of the possible times for these interactions.

Finally, remember that social interactions can be very tiring for children on the autism spectrum. While a number of strategies have been provided in this chapter to develop social skills, you also need to consider providing some space for the child to withdraw from any kind of social demands and relax.

Summary of the main points

- Difficulties in social behaviour could be linked to difficulties in developing a bond with the carer and lack of theory of mind.
- A variety of strategies can be used to develop some of these behaviours.
- It is important to concentrate on peer awareness and involving peers in supporting the child with autism for the child to be completely accepted in the setting.

Activity time

- Try watching a foreign language film without the subtitles and guess the storyline. Then you can turn on the subtitles to check yourself. Consider what helped you to make sense of the story. Which skills will an individual with autism need to do the same?
- Survey your setting to see how the rules are explained to the children. Discuss with your colleagues too. Are the children always getting consistent rules? If not, what can the implications be for someone with autism?
- Meet with the family to identify which of the social behaviours they consider important and plan your intervention accordingly.

Useful websites

Intensive Interaction: www.intensiveinteraction.co.uk/
Options programme: www.option.org
TEACCH: www.teacch.com
Transporters software: www.thetransporters.com

CHAPTER

5

Communication

Communication is often the area that alerts parents as well as early years practitioners that something is different about a child. Communication includes not just speech, but the various means that we use to pass our message to others, such as gestures, body language, written communication, and signs and symbols. Generally most of us feel a need to communicate and have a basic understanding of what is involved in this process. Therefore we are able to communicate well as long as we have speech and understand the language that is being used. Because of this inborn ability to communicate it is hard for us to appreciate that the ability to speak does not always lead to better communication skills in children with autism. This is particularly relevant when working with parents of a child on the spectrum, as they sometimes believe that if their child learns to speak everything will get better. This is especially so where the child has regressed and stopped talking, or shows exceptional skills in other areas, which parents believe showcase their child's 'normal' abilities. You need to explain in a sensitive manner that children with autism can find it difficult to communicate even if they develop speech. However, it is possible to teach some skills for communication to all children on the autism spectrum.

The kind of difficulties that a child with autism can have include delay or lack of development of speech where he does not compensate with any other means of communication. He may also find it difficult to initiate or sustain a conversation. Where the child does have speech, he may use it in a limited or a repetitive way, with some use of idiosyncratic words and phrases (WHO 2007). It is in these children with developed language and speech skills that the communication impairments become more evident. In fact Noens and van Berckelaer-Onnes (2004) state that the main problem that children with autism have is with communication rather than language; this implies that interventions should focus more on this aspect than developing speech.

As the main purpose of communication is sharing information there have to be at least two people involved for it to be effective. For example, this book has not reached its communicative intention until it has been read by someone. A successful communication often requires fine-tuning between two or more individuals where they are trying to pass on information to each other, trying to make sense of the other person's message and clarify when they do not understand it. As can be seen, this is a complicated process and needs a basic understanding that others may not know the information you have to share, as well as the ability to empathize with the emotions and feelings that the narrator is sharing – or, in other words, a theory of mind. Lack of or delay in developing this can be attributed as one of the causes for the difficulties that children with autism face in the area of communication, especially when it comes to reading between the lines.

Theoretical understanding

Williams et al. (2001) suggest a biological explanation for the difficulties in imitation skills or understanding other people's state of mind. They say that this is because of dysfunctional mirror neurons. Mirror neurons get activated when we are involved with an action or see someone else engaged in the same action. This enables us to imagine how someone else will be feeling in that situation. There are currently studies being carried out to understand the fuller implications of this on developing skills in people on the autism spectrum.

Another theory which can contribute to understanding some of the difficulties is the weak central coherence theory proposed by Frith in 1989. She stated that while people with autism pay a lot of attention to the detail, they tend to miss the overall meaning of the information. This could influence areas such as language comprehension and understanding of social rules as they are paying attention to specific situations but not realizing the common basis of these situations. Frith (1989) suggested this also explains why some people with autism are good at skills which require a focus on detail. However, this theory does not explain the reason for this ability to focus on detail and has been challenged by some other academics. Happe and Frith (2006) have since stated that not everyone on the spectrum has difficulty in understanding the whole, but they do seem to prefer to concentrate on the detail.

Although it may not be completely satisfactory, weak central coherence theory does highlight that children with autism are better at taking information from one source and in detail. Their difficulty in processing multidimensional information can make communication and interaction difficult as there is a lot of information to take from different sources. Some researchers, such as Rapin and Dunn (2003), state that this makes it difficult for some people on the autism spectrum to process sound and vocabulary-related information. This is one of the reasons that using visual means, where they have more time to process the information, can help in communication. Visual means could be signs, gestures, symbols, written words, pictures and objects.

Communication assessment

Before any intervention is started, it is necessary to have an understanding of the child's communication abilities. If your setting has access to a speech and language therapist they will usually be able to conduct a formal assessment. However, by using informal assessments you will be able to gather some information to enable you to select appropriate strategies. As children with autism have difficulties in generalizing skills from one situation to another, it is best if you gather information during different activities, with different people and from the home setting as well. The kind of information you are looking for during your observations is:

- How does the child respond to any given instruction?
- How does the child express that he requires something?
- How does he refuse or express his displeasure?
- How does the child initiate a conversation or seek information?
- How does the child respond to routine social greetings?

The idea is to get a good understanding of the child's ability to express himself (sometimes called expressive communication) and how he understands others' communication (receptive skills). Do not ignore unconventional means used by the child such as pulling an adult to an object, crying, or throwing something away. Sometimes children could be communicating more via such non-verbal means than by speaking.

It is possible that some of the children you are working with come from families where more than one language is spoken. In such situations you want to gather information about how they communicate in the other language(s). Bilingualism or even multilingualism is a norm in a number of countries and cultures. There is no evidence to suggest that children will find it difficult to learn a second language (Cummins 1984) as long as they have the skills to learn one language; there is no need, therefore, to discourage parents from using a second language at home. It is possible that some younger children with autism may be confused about which language to use with whom. For example, some children from a south Asian background tend to speak to me in their first language, assuming that I will understand it as I look similar culturally. However, most children will be able to differentiate after some time. A number of strategies which are used with children with autism, such as using visuals, are just as applicable for children with a second language (Curtis 1992).

Whether the child speaks only one language or more, children usually have better ability at understanding any given language than using it. This does not seem to be the case with children on the autism spectrum. Hudry et al. (2010) suggest that in these children language comprehension can lag behind their expressive language. Therefore, we should not assume that a child will be able to understand the same level of language as he uses. It also highlights the importance of focusing on developing language comprehension or receptive language, as unless the child is able to understand the words he is unlikely to use them appropriately.

Developing receptive communication

Some people with autism such as Temple Grandin (1995) and a number of professionals in the field of autism (Hodgdon 1995; Jordan and Powell 1995; Quill 1995) state that using visual means can be effective while communicating with children with autism. This could be because visuals tend to be static and therefore can be referred back to, and the need to understand spoken language is minimal. A number of visual means can be used throughout the day in early years settings to clarify information. Hodgdon (1995) states that people with autism demonstrate better understanding and participation when their environments are visually enriched. Visual information can also help in providing consistency between the various people interacting with the child if they agree on what the symbol or picture card comprises, and repeat the same thing. This can be important for some children in the initial stages when they may not respond to different terms being used to represent the same message.

Using principles from the TEACCH programme (Schopler and Reichler 1983) can help with receptive language and understanding the world. TEACCH structures the physical environment so that a person with autism can understand what to do, where to do it, when and for how long. They use designated areas within the setting, such as having a book corner or a play corner, to explain what the child is expected to do in that area. Visual timetables are used to explain the sequence of the day or the activity. It is considered to be a good idea to provide individual timetables to begin with so that the child can refer to it as many times as required. Similarly, children are clearly informed when an activity is finished. It has been suggested that using symbols like this can help reduce the child's anxiety as well as helping him to understand the structure and routines (Peeters 1997). Visual cues and picture schedules can also decrease the child's dependence on adults and develop his independence.

Ross's mother is confused about her son. She explains to the speech and language therapist that he seems to choose when he wants to follow an instruction. After observing their interaction for some time the speech therapist realizes that it was the way the instructions were being given which produced the differences. Ross seems to follow the instruction when his name is called at the beginning of the sentence but not when it comes later on in the sentence, such as 'Come here Ross'.

People with autism find it difficult to shift their attention from one topic to another or from one activity to another due to their brain abnormalities (Courchesne 1989). This could be the reason why Ross was inconsistent in his reaction as by the time he attends to his name there is no instruction to follow. While using visuals can help with this process to an extent, it is nevertheless important to ensure you get the child's attention before you give the information –for example by tapping on their shoulder or calling their name.

Another difficulty that some children with autism have is in processing information quickly. This could mean that they take longer to react than we expect. Most of us will naturally reframe the instruction and repeat it to make it easy for them to understand. However, children with autism could find this unhelpful as they will treat this as a new piece of information and start the whole process of understanding again. A better strategy to use will be to give an instruction and then wait for some time (I generally say count to ten in your head). If the child has not reacted to your instruction by this time, treat it as if they have not understood it. Take the child through the motions of the instruction by emphasizing the key words: for example, 'shoes, shoes off'. Similarly, when the child drags or leads you to something he wants, name it before giving it to the child.

Simplifying your sentences in this way will give the child a better chance of making a connection between the words and their corresponding objects and actions. Try to build up the sentences using fewer words but keep them grammatically correct so that when the child is ready to imitate he has correct examples to follow. Some able and verbal children may also need this approach when they are anxious in a situation. Strategic pausing can be used along with simplified sentences to encourage the child to initiate communication. For example, build a routine for an activity, such as saying 'ready, steady, go' before you push a car and then slowly start waiting before you say 'go' for the child to say it.

Quill (1995) suggests that for a child to initiate communication it is important that he has a reason to do so. When adults are anticipating all the child's needs, or where all the material is accessible for the child, there is very little need for him to request anything. I am aware that many early years practitioners are keen to develop the child's independence and will find not providing accessible material as contrary to early years philosophy. Although you may not want to do it on every occasion, sabotaging or engineering situations can actually contribute to naturalistic learning of communication skills.

Sussman (2004) suggests a number of such ideas in her book for parents, which can equally be tried by practitioners. Some of the possible ideas include:

- During the snack time, give the snack only to children who ask for it.
- Put a favourite object out of reach, which the child can see but cannot reach.
- Behave in a different way from the expected behaviour, e.g. collect your apron for painting, but then go to the book corner.
- Do not provide an item that is required to complete an activity, e.g. brushes for a painting activity.

These situations must appear natural and as genuine 'mistakes'. Make sure you change them around and do them randomly so that the child does not start thinking that this is part of the activity routine!

Developing expressive communication

Quill (1995) provides some basic prerequisites for becoming an effective communicator. She states that it is important for the children to understand the relationship between cause and effect. They also need to have a desire to communicate. They need to have someone to communicate with where they have something to communicate about. This means that they need receptive adults and peers who are willing to engage with them. Finally they need a means of communication. As mentioned in this chapter and the previous one, the means of communication does not have to be speech alone. This section will provide some strategies where these principles will be reiterated. The ideas are mostly based on incidental teaching which takes place in the natural setting.

Using interaction approaches as explained in the last chapter can help the child to understand the cause and effect principles as he realizes that he is controlling your behaviour. He also understands what he needs to do for you to react. Children with autism tend to communicate more to express their needs rather than for social interaction. Therefore, focus on using these needs to start developing skills such as requesting. Use a range of activities which are motivating for the child. This could be a chasing game or singing a song. Introduce these and build a routine. Once you feel that the child understands the game or has learnt the actions or words for the song, use pauses and wait for the child to fill in the gaps. Similarly, tickling, rough and tumble games, or wind-up toys can all be used – you do not repeat the game unless the child indicates he wants you to continue. Dyer and Luce (1996) have suggested that these time delay methods can be very effective in helping the child to initiate requests.

Pre-verbal skills

> After Jo has had her turn on the bike, Sue gives it to another child saying 'Harpreet's turn'. Jo makes the sign for more as she wants to have another ride. Because Sue has her back turned to Jo, she does not see this request. After making the sign again, Jo in her frustration goes and pushes Harpreet from the bike to have another turn.

Children have to understand that they need to seek someone's attention before communicating to them to avoid such frustration and behaviour. Even if the child is non-verbal he needs to learn to tap the other person or use other appropriate means to gain their attention. Verbal children can be taught to call the person's name by modelling this behaviour.

Turn-taking is another vital skill to engage in communication. This can be taught using similar principles as those used to teach waiting skills. Use a visual clue that will help the child to understand when it will be his turn. This could be passing on a bean bag, handing over a cap or block, throwing dice, or a visual timetable. Introduce this in a one-to-one situation and keep the waiting period fairly short to begin with. Once he is able to take turns with one person, introduce another person but reduce the time to wait for the turn. Games where there is a natural turn-taking process, such as chasing games, can also be used.

The number of children with autism who do not have any speech or have lost their ability to speak is variously estimated by different sources as ranging from 20 to 60 per cent. Providing an alternative means of communication is therefore important for this group. Even some verbal children find it useful to have these as part of their total communication skills so that they can use them in case they cannot remember a word or are unable to speak because of their anxiety.

Augmentative alternative communication systems, as they are called, could include using sign language, using symbols or pictures, or using voice-generating aids including computers. The decision about which method to use has to be based on the individual child's requirements. The strength of sign language is its flexibility, though Jordan and Powell (1995) argue that the symbolic nature of sign language can make it difficult for children with autism to learn and use it effectively. Difficulties with imitation and motor planning can also be an issue, although some individuals are able to use it for certain communicative functions. Picture-based and voice-generating aids are becoming more popular because of this. Also, neither of these need the communicative partners to learn a different language, so this widens the scope of people the child can interact with. An additional advantage of pictorial or symbol systems is that for children who are bilingual, the picture can be named in both the languages, thereby enabling the child to communicate with his family members as well as the wider society.

Using pictures for communication

Although pictures are generally accessible for most children, some may be unable to associate a picture to the real object and you may have to start with the real objects or miniature versions. Routines can again be a good way to introduce these in an early years setting. For example, develop a routine of putting on an apron for water play. As the child gets used to this routine, take away the aprons and place a photo or symbol of an apron there instead. When the child picks this up, immediately intervene and say 'apron' and hand it to him. Once the child starts associating the picture with the apron, move further away and let the child find an adult or a peer to make the request. Set more such routines so that the number of pictures or symbols the child uses can expand.

A more formal approach to a similar method is called Picture Exchange Communication System (PECS) (Bondy and Frost 1994). PECS is based on the behaviourist principles and aims to teach spontaneous and functional communication. PECS has various stages which are taught to the child in a graded fashion. Although the last stage does cover some elements of commenting, the main focus of PECS is teaching requesting skills for a desired item. This approach does need two adults at the initial stages. According to Bondy and Frost (1994), PECS helps in the development of speech in some children with autism. However, in an analysis of various studies that evaluated PECS, Flippin et al. (2010) have found that speech did not develop in all children. They also found that evidence for maintenance of the initial improvements in PECS is not always consistent. This is perhaps because the settings or the family are inconsistent in using the system. It is important that once an alternative means of communication is provided to the child, this should always be to hand and its use encouraged. Whether or not all children develop speech, PECS seems to help children with no or limited language skills in understanding the structure of language (Gordon et al. 2011).

> Amar was new to the nursery and was quite happy to play with the new toys. When the nursery staff thought he had settled well, they went to encourage him to play with some play dough. Amar hates touching any soft objects, and as soon as he saw the play dough, he toppled the table and tried to bite the member of staff who brought the dough.

This case study highlights the importance of teaching a child to say no in a socially appropriate way. This is one of the essential skills for children with autism to learn, along with saying yes. Start by using something that the child does not like, like play dough in Amar's case. Take it close to him and offer it. If the child uses symbols for communication, place a symbol for 'no' close to him. While one adult is offering Amar play dough, the other member of staff can help him pick the symbol and give it to the person with the play dough. On receiving the symbol the other adult could acknowledge it with 'Oh, you don't want it' and take the unpleasant thing away. If the child is verbal, then use modelling to show the correct response before he is offered the object. Pairing the visual or the verbal response along with shaking the head to convey the message can help when the child's symbol card is not available. It is necessary that initially the response is honoured in every instance so that the child understands the power of the sign, symbol or word. Once this happens, the 'no' sign can also be used to explain when a choice is not available for the child.

Echolalia

Some children with autism could be repeating words or phrases, which is known as echolalia. This can be immediately after something has been said or after some time gap. This may not be new for you as an early years practitioner as most children do engage in this behaviour around the age of two, generally to help them in learning the language. What is unusual in autism is that some children could be using echolalia even after this age.

> Damien goes to Shanice (who is on a work experience) and says to her 'you want biscuit?' She finds this very cute but politely refuses it, but Damien persists with his offer and she reluctantly accepts. But rather than going and getting her a biscuit, Damien keeps repeating the same phrase, which confuses her. James, Damien's key worker, comes and gives him a biscuit and explains to her that when Damien says the phrase he is actually requesting a biscuit!

As can be seen in the above example, echolalia can be used by children on the autism spectrum for communicative purposes. It is important to understand what purpose the child is using the phrase or word for. Along with a range of other reasons, the child could also be repeating phrases when he is anxious. Detailed observations can help you to some extent, but again working in collaboration with the family can give you a better insight. Research has indicated that increase in the rate of echolalia is found when children cannot follow the language. In such cases it is the communicational partners who need to change their style of communication by simplifying it and using visual supports, as explained above. It is tempting to think that since the child is able to repeat long phrases he understands such complicated language. Often children with autism may not understand the relevance of individual words and treat the whole phrase as a single word.

To reduce such misunderstanding and to share the information among all the adults supporting the child, a communication dictionary can be developed. This could provide information on the phrases the child uses and what they could mean.

Example of a communication dictionary:

What the child does or says	What it means
Damien says 'you want a biscuit?'	It can mean that he is hungry and wants a snack.
When Damien is asked to go out to play and he says 'it's wet play', or when he says this in the playground.	He means that he wants to be inside or by himself.

Once the function is understood, accept the words or phrases as if they represent the same request. But rather than fulfilling the request for that phrase, model the appropriate one. So, in the above example, James could have said 'I want biscuit' while handing the biscuit to Damien. When information is provided in this fashion in a meaningful context, children tend to learn the new phrases and start using them in specific situations. This is why it is important to not add words such as 'say, I want…', as the child will start repeating the whole sequence. If the child is repeating because they are anxious, however, then what is needed is reassurance.

Reversal of pronouns

Some children with autism confuse pronouns such as 'you' and 'I', and may even use their own names to refer to themselves. For example, Henna says, 'Henna wants to play'. As we have seen in the previous chapter, according to Hobson (1993) and Jordan and Powell (1995) this could be because the child has not developed self-awareness. Other reasons could be that the child is echoing what they have heard, when others use 'you' or their name to address them. It could also be because children with autism find it difficult to understand the changing references, which are not logical to them.

With some children, simply modelling the behaviour with explicit emphasis can help. Others may need more concrete strategies such as using photographs. Gather photographs of the child and yourself doing the same activities. Share these with the child and model 'I am...' when referring to your picture. Then show the child his picture and allow him to copy your phrase. Some children find it useful to actually have the word 'I' under their photo as a visual reminder. Slowly stop modelling and just point to the word, and later take away the word as well. Once the child has learnt to use the pronoun with the pictures, prompt him to use it in other situations as well. Only later should you start on a different pronoun.

Idioms and metaphors

When we say 'wash your hands in the toilet' do we actually mean that? I know a woman with autism who says that is exactly what she did as a child when instructed by the teachers. We use a number of phrases where the child has to understand the intention rather than the literal meaning. As some children have difficulties in understanding these intentions, it makes it difficult for them to understand idioms or metaphors which are used in day-to-day life. It is advised to not use such phrases with children on the spectrum.

While this is fine to an extent, it is also necessary to teach them to understand such phrases for them to be part of society. The meaning of common phrases can be explained to the child. Pictorial depictions can be used to clarify the meaning by having a literal interpretation and one which shows the intended meaning. There is considerable material available on the market which does all this hard work for you.

With more able children, comic strip conversations can be used to do the same thing, related to the child's life. Carol Gray, who developed this idea, suggests that this can help the child to understand social situations. Line drawings are used to explain the situation while discussing it with them to explain how they perceived the situation and what an alternative explanation could be. I have used this method also to explain to children when it is fine to think something (such as 'she is a fat woman') but not appropriate to say it.

Explaining concepts

If somebody says the word 'cat' do you need to go through pictures of every single cat to understand which one I am referring to? Most probably not, because you understand the concept of the word. Some people with autism find this difficult, because as far as they can see each individual cat is different and they are unable to understand which one the other person is referring to. Temple Grandin (1995) provides an insight into how people with autism acquire concepts, based on her own way of learning. She explains how different the patterns of learning are in people who are on the spectrum. Therefore, when introducing any concept it is important to highlight what makes this into a specific category – for example, by explaining how a cat is different from a tiger or a dog even though all of them have four legs and a tail. It is also a good idea to use pictorial representations of various cats so that the child does not think that only a Siamese cat is called a cat.

Some of the concepts which are taught in early years settings, such as sizes, are relative, and therefore difficult to understand for a child with autism. It is advisable to start with absolute concepts, such as 'full' and 'empty'. Children with autism seem to find it easier to understand one concept before understanding the opposite one. So present empty in all settings, and consolidate it before moving on to introducing full, or vice versa.

When introducing and assessing such concepts pay particular attention to the language you use and the clues you are providing. For example, when introducing positional words such as 'on' and 'in', make sure that the situation you set up enables you to establish that the child has in fact understood the concept of position and not just recognized the objects: for example, if you have a cup and a saucer and ask the child to put a lemon in the cup, the child may do this because he understood the word 'cup' and followed the logical action. Instead, if you have two cups, one of which is turned upside down, and then give the same instruction or ask the child to place it on the cup, as both the objects are the same it is easier to recognize if the child did understand the concept or not.

Conversational skills

Conversations generally involve a number of social skills along with cognitive and communicative ones. One of the key skills required is being able to recollect what has happened and share it with other people. Due to their lack of self-awareness some children with autism may find it easier to narrate what happened to others (Jordan and Powell 1995). You can start with situations where the child can retell what others did during an activity; along with this, work on self-recollection as well. It is easier to remember when the evidence is still available. Therefore, if you made some sandwiches, ask the children to remember what they did before you start the cleaning up. Having the material around can help as a visual reminder.

To develop recollection after a gap, digital cameras can be used to take pictures of the child performing various activities; then ask them towards the end what they did on that day, using the photographs as a reminder. It is also possible to share these with the family via email so that they get a good understanding of the routine and can have a conversation. If this is not possible, collect the wastage from the different activities the child was involved in and send it home in a container. Having the painting, the empty juice carton and so on can again act as a visual reminder. With some children, having pictures on a piece of paper for them to circle or write the events in their own words can serve a similar purpose.

To be able to engage in general conversation it is important to listen to what others are saying and take turns to share information. Active listening can be encouraged by using games such as 'Simon says', where the child can only follow the instruction if the phrase 'Simon says' is used. Games such as 'Guess what I have' can also be used. Here a child or an adult gets an object and the other members in the group have to ask questions to find out what the object is. Children could be provided with a list of areas that they may cover to seek the needed information, such as colour, material, purpose of use. This helps in developing purposeful questioning skills.

Example of a grid for asking appropriate questions:

What colour is the object?
What material is it made of?
What do you use it for?
What shape is it?

Providing similar grids or rules for turn-taking in conversations can also help in peer interactions. For example, explain to the child that they can say three things about their favourite topic and then ask the other person about their interest. Although this can be a bit formulaic, it could form the first steps for some children to work towards social communication and interaction with their peers.

Summary of the main points

- You, as a communication partner, have an important role in helping the child with autism to develop in this area, as receptive communication is a specific area of need for these children.
- Using visual strategies along with simplified language can be beneficial for a child with autism.
- Providing a good understanding of metaphors and concepts is important for developing the communication skills of the child.
- Remember to always generalize the learnt skills and involve peers wherever you can.

Activity time

- Make an assessment of a child with autism and one without autism to find out how they communicate. Observe what means the child without autism uses to communicate. Think of how you could develop similar skills with the child with autism.
- Make a list of activities and objects that the child seems to be engaging with the most. Consider how you could use these to develop communication skills (such as sabotage or introduction of a picture communication system).
- If you work with a child who is bilingual or multilingual, make a communication dictionary which has the words that the child says in the other language and their meaning. This can help everyone in your setting in case the child does use some of these words with one of you.

Useful websites

Carol Gray's website: www.thegraycenter.org
Picture Exchange Communication System: www.pecs.org.uk
Printable symbols: www.do2learn.com/picturecards/overview.htm
www.mrsriley.com

6

Play and flexible thinking

Play is central to what we do in early years settings and is often the time when children show enjoyment and you can hear laughter. Jordan (2003) comments that play not only enables children to learn about people and social situations but also encourages them to be with others. According to Vygotsky (1978), this shared experience of engaging in pretend play helps them to develop an understanding of the social and cultural values of their society. He further argues that when children are engaged in symbolic play it contributes to the development of their memory, and their logical and abstract thinking. Therefore, when children with autism are not engaged in social play, they lose the opportunity to develop a variety of skills. Although difficulties in the area of play and flexible thinking have been part of the criteria for autism since its inception, there is comparatively limited research on this subject. This chapter tries to synthesize some of the existing research as well as providing some practical strategies which can be used when working with children on the autism spectrum.

Carol is unable to think how to engage Aisha in any play activity. Aisha often sits in the corner of the playground and feels the leaves. Sometimes she lifts them up and looks at the sky with them. She seems to be happy engaged in this, and can spend any amount of time there. In fact, sometimes it is a challenge to get her into the nursery and engage her in any other activity.

Should Carol be worried about Aisha? This will depend on how we describe play or what we understand it to be. Wolfberg (2009) compiled a few of the salient points that she thinks are necessary for any activity to be classified as play. According to her, play is fun time for children, in which they are actively engaged. It is an activity that is child-centred and is chosen by them because of their own inner motivation for it. Unlike some of the other tasks that children are engaged with, the focus of the play is often on the process itself rather than reaching an end. Finally, play tends to be flexible, where children experiment with various aspects and storylines and make sense of their world. On the basis of this description Aisha is engaged in play as she is enjoying herself, engrossed in the activity she has selected and does not seem to have any end goal that she is aiming for. Then what is the reason for Carol's unease? Perhaps an understanding of the developmental stages of play will answer this question.

Cognitive stages of play

There are some generally agreed stages of play that all children go through, which can be broadly divided as: sensory-motor stage, exploratory stage, pretend or functional play and symbolic play. Each of these areas will be briefly described here.

One of the first play stages that all newborn babies engage in is called the sensory-motor stage. Children at this stage are basically interacting with all the sensory information they are receiving and understanding it. They often react with joy when adults interact with them physically, such as being tickled, rocked and swung around. Other senses are also used where they are touching, smelling or licking things. It seems like Aisha is involved at this stage of play.

In the exploratory stage, children are trying to understand the properties of different materials. Therefore they manipulate them in an advanced fashion, such as stacking objects over each other, trying to open bottles and doors and doing puzzles. Children start to get an understanding of their own role in controlling things and that reactions can be sought in this way.

During pretend or functional play children tend to re-enact situations they have seen in their daily life, such as cooking food, talking on a phone or driving a bus while making a 'brrm' sound. Children are using a real object or its miniature for its actual purpose. They often actively seek interaction with others in this stage by involving them in their play scripts.

Symbolic play is the next step of pretend play, as children start using unrelated objects as if they mean something different. Leslie (1987) described three forms of symbolic play. The first one was object substitution, where an object is used for something else – such as using a book as if it is a computer. Then children may start attributing false properties as if they exist. This could be when they pretend the food tastes nice or the doll is ill, etc. At the third stage children start making reference to an absent object as if it is present, such as pretending to drive their car over an imaginary bridge or rail track. In the symbolic stage, children also move further than just replicating situations from their lives and use more imaginative situations such as mermaids, fairies and superheroes. It is considered that the ability to substitute one object for another at this stage helps the child with abstract thinking (Vygotsky 1978). Therefore, children start to understand that symbols such as written and verbal words can represent objects and events and can be used for this purpose when communicating with others.

Social play

Play is not just a cognitive process but also involves different levels of social interaction. Children generally start with the orientation stage, where they are aware of the presence of another child or adult. Children may look at this other person or their play material but do not actually engage with them in any way. Some children with autism find even accepting the presence of others difficult and may need a graded introduction to this. With young children who do not mind physical contact, starting with rough and tumble games with a certain amount of predictability, such as tickling, can help them in accepting others and may even lead to the next stage.

In parallel play children start playing alongside the other person, sometimes sharing but at other times having their own material. The focus is more on having a shared space and being involved in a similar activity. Being with another child or adult enables the child to see other ways to use the material and different play scripts to their own, and can help them to move to the next stage of cognitive play. Interaction-based approaches in autism, such as Options or Intensive Interaction are usually working at this stage of social play.

The third stage is the cooperative stage, where children start sharing their play materials and involve each other in their activities. This is the stage that adults often think of as play. Children tend to communicate to each other by asking for the material or providing suggestions to each other. This stage involves active turn-taking as children show awareness of the others and are willing to be flexible in their play schemes. This would require them to have some theory of mind skills. Although it is not completely clear from the case study, it appears as if Aisha is not even working at the orientation stage of social play. The reason Carol is worried about her is perhaps because of this lack of social awareness rather than cognitive play skills as such.

Play and autism

A majority of children with autism are able to engage in the sensory-motor and exploratory stages of play, as Aisha in the case study did. Some children may also show pretend and symbolic play, although this still raises some contradictions in the field. Paterson and Arco (2007) comment that young children with autism tend to be involved in play activities that are repetitive and ritualistic, and lack imaginative themes. This view is also shared by Baron-Cohen (1987), who found that although children with autism were able to engage in pretend play, their ability to do so was impaired compared to children with other learning difficulties or children with no disabilities. However, not everyone agrees with this idea. For example, Lewis and Boucher (1988) found in their research that children with autism are able to pretend if they are given some ideas to build on. Similarly, Jarrold (2003) found that even though children with autism may not be able to pretend by themselves, they seem to understand when someone else pretends. All these researchers, in their own different ways, are arguing that the ability to pretend and understand pretence is not completely impaired in children with autism.

Leslie (1987) tried to explain the reason for the difficulties that children with autism have in pretend play. According to him, pretend play involves a complex representational stance. During pretend play, the child needs to simultaneously show an understanding of the real purpose of the object while also remembering its newly assigned identity. In his research, Leslie found that children with autism had difficulties in holding these identities in their minds. Although Leslie calls it pretend play, what he is actually referring to is symbolic play here.

> When all the children were asked to come back into the class for story time, Shola came along with the others. However, while other children were able to settle down quickly, Shola was still pretending to be the policeman and trying to catch the thieves.

In this scenario, Shola must have been able to hold the two identities when he started playing the game with his peers. This means that not all children with autism are unable to engage in symbolic play either. Ungerer and Sigman (1981) argue that it is not as if children with autism are unable to engage in symbolic play, but their ability to engage in this seems to be correlated to their levels of understanding and using language. This leads back to the argument of symbolic play contributing to abstract thinking and vice versa. What Shola is finding difficult here is also understanding when the play has finished and they are all back to their real identities. Children with autism generally seem to cope well when there is a clear ending to a game but find it more difficult when this is not the case, or the game has been abruptly stopped, as here, before they are ready for it.

The unpredictable nature of play can make it more difficult for some children with autism to engage in play or any activity which requires them to be flexible, and they may instead focus on more predictable routines or play schemes. Children sometimes may exhibit pretend play but may be using the same script every time. This could be one reason why some researchers have found that social play in these children is restricted, with some preferring more solitary activities compared to other children with disabilities (Watson et al. 2003).

There are a number of other possible reasons that different theorists have posited to explain the difference in flexible thinking and play skills found in children with autism.

Theory of mind

Jordan and Powell (1995) argue that it is not that children with autism lack imagination, but what they find difficult is flexibility of thinking. Some can show imaginative skills in situations that are not play-related. The reason cooperative play involving functional or symbolic play is difficult for children with autism is because it requires a higher level of understanding of the theory of mind. To be able to engage in these games the child needs to be able not only to predict what the characters may do or feel in a certain situation but also to change his responses on the basis of how the other child or adult develops their own character.

Empathizing and systemizing theory

This builds on the theory of mind idea. Lawson et al. (2004) state that while people with autism may have difficulties in understanding others and empathizing with their feelings, they have good ability to analyse or construct systems. This need to systemize could mean that the person wants to keep everything the same, making the world predictable. It is argued that this could be the reason for the narrow interests, repetitive behaviours, and wanting sameness which are seen in people with autism. This is also given as the reason why people with autism have difficulty in generalizing what they have learnt in one situation to a new one, because for them it is a different system.

Executive function difficulties

Executive function involves the ability to plan and problem-solve to achieve a future goal. This ability is controlled by the frontal lobes in our brains (Ozonoff 1995). Difficulties in this area could mean problems in planning and shifting attention, and difficulties in being flexible in their thoughts. This could lead to a situation where the individual is unable to move away from repetitive and ritualistic behaviours and may develop strong, narrow interests. Currie and Ravenscroft (2002) argue that these narrow interests can impact the child's ability to consider another person's viewpoint, which could in turn influence his ability to pretend. Some academics have argued that even though not all people with autism have difficulties in their frontal lobes, they still seem to have difficulties in executive functions, which could be the reason for the limited play skills and the repetitive and ritualistic behaviours. Adults with autism, such as Grandin (1995), also comment that they tend to follow routines as they are unsure of anything new. Others argue that executive function difficulties seen in people with autism are also seen in other conditions and therefore cannot be used as an explanation of difficulties seen in this population (Bishop 1993). Hill (2004) further adds that the difficulties in this area could be related to learning difficulties rather than autism per se. Although this theory does not explain why people with autism show executive function difficulties, it provides a theory why certain activities related to flexible thinking are more difficult for people on the autism spectrum.

In addition to these three, Frith (2003) argues that weak central coherence can also lead to limited pretend play or repetitive behaviours, as the child is focusing on a part of the object, such as the wheels of the car, and not actually looking at the whole of the car. Even though there are different possible avenues which can be followed for interventions, based on your own theoretical position, it is clear that flexible thinking and play are interconnected and that strategies which are being used would need to address both aspects.

Assessment of play skills

Although the stages of play have been presented as developmental in this chapter, it is necessary to understand that children with autism do not always progress in clear developmental profiles. It is possible that the child could be at different levels of play in different settings or with different material. Assessing the child's play skills will enable you to get a clearer picture of his abilities. Since play is supposed to be child-centred and child-led, having an insight into the likes and dislikes of the child would also help you to individualize the strategies. You can use any assessment tool for noting your observations. The main information you need to gather is the level of cognitive play and social play the child is involved at and the activity or location where this is taking place.

A sample of a play observation sheet:

	Peer awareness	Parallel play	Cooperative play	Location/ activity
Sensory-motor				
Exploratory				
Pretend/ functional				
Symbolic				

Strategies which can be used

Since flexibility of thinking seems to be important for play as well as daily living, introducing this in a graded fashion can be helpful. Using principles of TEACCH can help in providing some structure and predictability for the child. Having predictable routines will reduce the need for the child to develop his own routines and rituals as there is already an existing system. This can be provided by using a visual timetable for the day or the activity, but could also be having a clear beginning and ending for each session. This will prepare the child for the current activity at the beginning and the new one towards the end. Having such structure will help the child to move from one activity to the other more easily. Along with helping the child with predictability, these same routines can also be used to introduce flexibility. Once the child feels comfortable with an activity which has clear starting and ending points, you can start introducing new elements in the middle. For example, you might always start the day in your setting with a hello song and then a group activity, followed by choice time: in which case you could start changing the nature of the group activity so that it is singing on some days, a small story on others, or even group playtime. As the session still has some familiarity it is easier for children on the spectrum to cope with the unpredictable elements.

If you combine this with having a generic picture for group time on the visual timetable and then explain what the activity will be on the day, it will also help. Similarly, you can also introduce a symbol to represent change on the visual timetable. Initially try to keep these changes or surprises pleasant by making it something the child likes. Once he stops reacting to the change in a negative way, you can slowly have a variety of changes, including some non-preferred activities. Preparing the child in this way will help him to cope with all the regular changes which are part of an early years setting, such as staff changes, activity change, and wet play sessions. In general, children with autism are able to cope with changes better if they are prepared for them.

Going back to the basics of play, as research suggests, children with autism generally are able to engage in the sensory-motor and exploratory play situations. Exploratory play such as stacking cups or completing a puzzle is often logical and hence easy to comprehend for a child with autism. This section will therefore focus more on developing pretend play and symbolic play. There are primarily two different ways of encouraging play skills in children with autism; one involves direct teaching using behavioural principles of reward and shaping, and the other involves the more naturalistic way of scaffolding play.

Strategies based on behaviouristic principles are popular with some practitioners as they show immediate results. The research evidence has shown that children with autism are capable of engaging in pretend play if it is introduced in a structured way (Lewis and Boucher 1995). Pivotal Response Training is one such technique which is based on behaviouristic principles but is also child-centred and is usually implemented in a naturalistic environment rather than in a clinical setting. Stahmer (1995) used this approach in a study to develop symbolic play. Stahmer used an activity which was chosen by the child and demonstrated the expected play sequences. The child with autism was reinforced when correct responses were made and later on maintenance tasks were included for them to be generalized in regular play situations. According to Stahmer, Pivotal Response Training increased symbolic play routines in all the children with autism, who showed more complex sequences and also joined their peers in play situations.

Although behaviourist principles can be effective, critics argue that relying on very structured play approaches makes the child a respondent who performs what has been taught rather than making his own initiations (Wolfberg and Schuler 1993). However, one could argue that most of the pretend play that children initially engage in is re-enactment of day-to-day situations and therefore this will be the first step towards developing symbolic play. The danger I feel is more on the heavy structure which may be used. For example, in a small-scale research study, Boudreau and D'Entremont (2010) found that when repetitive video modelling was combined with reinforcers, children with autism showed less originality in their play and tried to copy the sequence that was modelled. Some would argue that this kind of play turns into an activity with a definite goal rather than exploring and experimenting.

Facilitated play, on the other hand, will gently take the child to the next stage of play based on their current repertoire. The adult may still demonstrate other ways that the object can be used or make additions to the play scheme that the child is using. Interaction approaches which were discussed in the previous chapters can be classified as fitting this approach. In a study conducted in an early years setting, Theodorou and Nind (2010) found that the adults can facilitate play by taking the role of a supporter of the child, mediating their interactions with peers, and sometimes by actively engaging in play. They felt that for social play to take place in an early years setting, it is important that the adults in the setting are working in a collaborative way, where they are supporting each other's attempts to encourage the child to play and engage with their peers. They also state that this is possible when the curriculum is flexible and play becomes a central aspect of it. The limitations of this approach are that it can be time-consuming and the child with autism may not be motivated in developing his play.

A study by Kok et al. (2002) with children in early years compared the effects of structured play versus facilitated play. They found that although children gave more communicative responses in structured play, they initiated communication more in a facilitated play situation. They also found that the cognitive ability of the child influenced how they learnt under the different approaches. Children with higher mental age were able to show more appropriate play and communication in a facilitated approach, though this was not the case for children with lower cognitive abilities. Due to these differences, Kok et al. (2002) conclude that a variety of approaches are required while working with children with autism, which need to be individualized for each child. This chapter takes this view and provides strategies which are based on a variety of theoretical positions.

Since one of the core difficulties that children on the autism spectrum have is social interaction, play at any level should aim to encourage their social play. It is not necessary that children have to reach the pretend or symbolic play stage for them to take part in parallel play or cooperative play. Even when children are at the exploratory stage and engaged in games with matching, sorting and puzzles these can be used as peer interactive games. You could encourage the children to play alongside each other sharing the material, and when the child with autism is able to accept it you could even start turn-taking and negotiation as part of this activity. For example, each child gets part of one of the two puzzles and all the children with the same puzzle will need to work together. It has been found that if children with autism are provided with appropriate physical challenges and given clear boundaries their social play and initiations can increase when they are engaged in motor play activities (Yuill et al. 2007).

While working on the social elements of play, you can work on the different cognitive stages of play. When encouraging the child to pretend play, it is better for some children if you can start this in the real situations for these activities. For example, if you want the child to learn to pretend cooking, having tea or a telephone conversation, it will be better to do these in the home corner. You can start with real objects and only pretend to eat or cook the invisible food, and then slowly move towards miniature versions. Some children may need modelling for them to imitate the actions. This would mean that both you and the child will need exactly the same set of items so that the child can see your actions and imitate them. Do emphasize that you are pretending, as this will help the child to differentiate between reality and pretence. Phillips and Beavan (2012) call this 'identiplay' and provide some scripts and strategies in their book.

Even after the child has learnt to pretend using the real objects, it will still be beneficial to use the miniature versions in the same setting. Start moving away from the setting once the child shows that he can show pretence with these toys or miniature versions. So, building on the cooking idea, you could encourage the child to cook with the utensils in the garden or on the table. You are slowly encouraging the child to understand the concept of symbolism. Some children may associate pretend play with only one set of toys and may not engage in pretend play with a different set. It is important therefore that generalization is built in from the start, and that you use a variety of objects and also encourage the family to do the same at home.

You can also start scaffolding the child's play by presenting him with choices or building on his responses. For example, you could ask the child 'Would you like to have orange juice or apple juice?' or give an attribute to the pretend object: 'This drink is hot.' When the child is able to copy such scripts then you could move them further on to symbolic play. Again, some children may need a more structured approach to begin with. Murdock and Hobbs (2011) conducted research involving small groups of children with autism and their peers without autism. They read a story to the group and then encouraged them to role-play it. As the children already had an existing script it was easy for children with autism to follow this and pretend to be a different person. After a few sessions the children were encouraged to extend some situations in the story. Scaffolding questions can be used for this purpose. Later on the children were presented with a new situation where a similar play script could be used. They found that children with autism were able to engage in such a play activity with adequate support.

Wolfberg and Schuler (1993) suggest a model of peer involvement which they call integrated play groups. Here children with and without autism are encouraged to play together in small groups. Usually the same sets of children meet on a regular basis in a natural setting to play, with the guidance of an adult facilitator. The idea is to support peer play by providing appropriate environment and support. The groups have a set opening and closing ritual and other visual prompts are provided as required. The adult starts with modelling the play sequences, then moves on to providing verbal prompts, and then is available for support but does not actively engage in the play (Wolfberg 2003). Practitioners using this approach state that this can be effective in facilitating play in children with autism. Most of the studies using this approach were conducted with older children, but I think the principles are applicable for younger children as well.

By involving peers they will be able to encourage the child with autism to move towards the next stage of play, such as symbolic play. Having peers will also ensure that the child is involved in a type of play that is socially appropriate for that group. The amount of guidance that is provided to the peers varies on the basis of the group needs. Some practitioners give basic clues to the peers, such as 'show him the picture card when you suggest a choice'. Some others have worked with the peers, explaining to them about differences and how the child with autism needs to be supported. How much support you are going to give the peers needs to be decided on the basis of your knowledge of the children involved.

Group games are yet another stage of play. Games with clearer roles and responsibilities are easier for children with autism to learn. Recent research using LEGO, where the child with autism and his peers are assigned specific roles such as builder, engineer and supplier, has been found useful in developing some social interaction (Owen et al. 2008). Here the children are provided with a sample of what the end product will be and a set of instructions. The engineer will provide these instructions to the other two children. The supplier provides the builder with the appropriate material and the builder actually implements the instructions for construction. It can be argued that since the focus is on an end product, this may not be classified as true play. However, unlike play, most games do have an end aim (such as winning the match) and this idea can prepare the child for such games. Other indoor games such as snakes and ladders or Uno can also be introduced as long as the child has the prerequisite skills, such as colour and number concepts. Simpler outdoor games with rules, such as a chase game, can also be introduced.

A key aspect with play and games for a child with autism is that these generally involve a lot of sensory input. Some children with autism find it difficult to cope with this as we will see in the next chapter. At such times they may react in a socially inappropriate way such as hitting the child who is shouting. It is necessary that the child is taught a socially appropriate way to get out of a situation when he finds it unbearable. This could be teaching and role-playing phrases like 'I want to have a break'.

Play and the playground can be stressful for children with autism because these situations demand the skills that they find difficult, such as communication, social skills and flexible thinking. However, as seen in the research, play also enables the development of these skills by practising them and learning from the reactions of the others. Having said that, sensory-motor play such as rocking or swinging can have a calming effect and it is necessary that children with autism are allowed to have opportunities to engage in this type of play if they wish to. We should not forget that play is supposed to be child-centred and pleasurable, and that everyone's idea of joy could be different.

Summary of the main points

- Children with autism can be good at the initial stages of play but may find pretend and symbolic play more difficult.
- Pretend and symbolic play can be developed by using a combination of approaches for most children on the spectrum.
- Social play can also be challenging for these children and it is important that peer interaction is incorporated in play wherever possible.
- Engaging in play can help the children to practise their social and communication skills and encourages them to be flexible in their thinking.

Activity time

- Complete the play assessment for the child you are working with. Make a note of her or his interests and material that seems to motivate them. Consider how these can be used to develop the child's play.
- Assess your setting to consider how more play opportunities can be developed by structuring your setting, adapting your timetable and with careful planning of the curriculum.
- Think about how you will encourage the child you are working with to interact with his or her peers.

Useful website

Printable matching games and visual cards for play situations: www.autismbuddy.com

7 Sensory issues

Although Kanner (1943) and Asperger in 1944 (Frith 1991) noticed differences in the way children with autism reacted to sensory information, not a lot of research was focused on this subject until recently. A number of adults with autism have commented over the years how they perceive different sensations and the impact this has on them. There is an increasing awareness now that these experiences can play a major role in the way children on the autism spectrum learn and live in the world, as explained by Wendy Lawson:

> I appear to have very sensitive ears, eyes and skin. Certain noises very definitely 'hurt' my ears and certain lights 'hurt' my eyes. Strip lighting is one of the worst, and lights that flash. If the strip lights have a grid covering them then I cope with them better. I have an insatiable appetite for touch and love to feel the roof of my mouth, especially when I am either insecure or very secure! I love soft material and soft skin but I hate to feel my own skin against myself. This means that I need to wear pyjamas in bed or put the sheet between my legs so that they do not come into direct contact with each other. (Lawson 2001: 119)

What Lawson describes here are sensory perception difficulties, which are sometimes known as sensory integrative disorders. These happen when the brain is unable to make sense of the sensations and organize them to understand the information (Ayres 1979). When we think of sensations we often think of our ability to see (visual), smell (olfactory), taste (gustatory), hear (auditory) and touch (tactile). Although these are considered as the primary sensations, there are two other sensations which are less well known – these are vestibular and proprioception. Our vestibular system provides us with a sense of balance. We are able to get this and maintain it through the liquid in the inner ear, which identifies the movement and position of the head. This is the reason why people experience disorientation when they have ear infections. The vestibular system helps us by providing information about speed and direction of movement. Proprioception provides us with body awareness. We gather this information through the muscles, tendons and joint movement. This is the sensation which informs us about the relative position of a certain body part, and about its movement. We are able to adjust and plan our body movements and apply appropriate pressure because of this. Difficulties in this area could lead to situations where, for example, a child is unable to navigate through a narrow space, or hold a can of juice.

The process of gathering the sensory information and providing the appropriate reactions is quite complex. The very first step that takes place is registering or becoming aware of the sensation. It is this awareness which alerts our brain. Our ability to register information is dependent on various factors such as our health condition, emotional state and our past experiences. For example, when you are sleeping in your bed and you feel someone gently touching you, you smile because you know that it is your child trying to wake you. When you experience a similar kind of touch at night in a dark alleyway you may react differently.

Once a sensation has been registered, we choose whether or not to react to it. We are making these choices, again, on the basis of our knowledge and experience of such situations. For instance, most people living on a main road will not respond when they hear the regular flow of traffic on the road, but may react when they hear a crash sound because that indicates a possible accident. Similarly, a child would generally respond to physical contact with pleasure, whereas if the child has been physically or sexually abused their reaction could be different. It is this kind of knowledge which helps us to organize our reactions to the sensation, which we then execute, whether that means rushing out to see what happened or running away from a danger. Although there are various stages in the whole process, we are doing this integration of the sensory input continuously throughout the day and often reacting to more than one sensation at the same time.

However, difficulties can arise at every step of this process, which can lead to unusual reactions as described by Lawson above. Ayres (1979) states that children with autism show sensory integrative dysfunctions. She suggests that some children have difficulties in being aware of the sensation, which can then result in them either overreacting or under-reacting to it. An overreaction could be when the child covers his ears when someone is talking, when he refuses to eat a food item which is mostly acceptable for others (such as tomatoes) because of its smell or texture, or where he refuses to have a haircut because of the sound of the scissors or being touched on the head. Sometimes these overreac-tions are described as hypersensitivity. Underreaction (or hyposensitiv-ity) to the sensation usually leads the child to seek that sensation. This could be the child who runs to a motorbike and places his ear near the engine, or a child who smells people, or a child who spins himself to get more vestibular stimulation. In fact, Delacato (1974) suggested that some of the behaviours associated with autism, such as self-stimulatory behaviours, are because of hyper or hyposensitivity to different sensa-tions. He suggested that children engage in these behaviours to nor-malize their sensory channels. What complicates this more is that the same individual could be hypersensitive to one sensation while being hyposensitive to another. It may also change on the basis of various other factors such as health, just as most people have a reduced ability to cope with sounds when they have a cold or an ear infection.

Some adults with autism have also commented that, due to their difficulties in being able to separate the different sources of information and choose the appropriate reaction, they try and process all the information they receive. Blake et al. (2003) have observed that some children in an educational setting may even find the movement of other children in the setting difficult to process and may bump into them or not move at all. Bogdashina (2003) suggests that since people with autism have such unusual sensory experiences, they may have different ways of processing the information. She thinks that some people may choose to concentrate on only one kind of sensation – sometimes called monotropic attention. This means that they choose to ignore other sensations and only register information from one source. This, of course, can also be beneficial as the person may show a good attention to detail for all the information they receive from that source. Bogdashina also refers to a condition known as synaesthesia, where the person may actually misunderstand information coming from the various senses: for example, they may perceive smell as sight.

Is this unique to autism?

There are some researchers and practitioners who are of the opinion that sensory differences should be included as one of the criteria for diagnosing autism. Others argue that these differences are not necessarily typical to people on the autism spectrum and that people with other types of disabilities or no disabilities could also be having difficulties in sensory perception. There has been some research in the field to judge how unique these differences are.

In a study conducted by Rogers et al. (2003) children with autism were compared with those with Fragile X syndrome and other developmental disabilities, as well as typically developing children. They found that children with Fragile X and autism showed more symptoms of sensory perception difficulties than the other two groups. These differences were mainly in the areas of touch, smell and taste, with some showing difficulties in filtering auditory information. Rogers et al. commented that children with autism also seem to have more pronounced difficulties in the areas of taste and smell compared to children with Fragile X syndrome. They also argued that these unusual responses to the sensory input seem to influence the stereotyped interests and behaviours found in children with autism. This research suggests that, although there are some sensory perception differences, these are not found only in children with autism.

In another study conducted by Leekam et al. (2007) children with autism were compared with those with language impairments and other developmental disabilities. They found that children with autism were more affected by sensory abnormalities than were children with language impairment and developmental disability. Children with autism differed from the comparison children both in the frequency and pattern of abnormalities. Leekam et al. argued that the children with autism were more likely to have dysfunctions across the range, whereas the other children tended to have difficulties mainly in one area. They concluded that almost 90 per cent of the children with autism in their study had sensory perception differences. Therefore, they argued that these differences are more common in children with autism than in others.

There is also an argument as to whether children with various levels of autism have different experiences. In the above mentioned study by Leekam et al. they found that the difference between children with low-functioning autism compared to their peers is not as significant as the difference in the children with high-functioning autism and their peers. If this is the case then it is possible that the level of sensory differences may be associated with the severity of learning difficulties rather than autism. However, Myles et al. (2004), in their study, found that there was no significant difference between the children with autism and those with Asperger syndrome in most areas other than with auditory processing. They suggested that the difficulties in this area could contribute to distractibility and inattention.

The current research is inconclusive as to whether there are significant differences between children with autism and those with Asperger syndrome and between all the children on the autism spectrum and those with or without other disabilities. In fact, we may all know of someone who has, or may even ourselves have, strong reactions to different sensations such as the screeching noise of a chair on the wooden floor, the texture of certain clothes or the smell of a specific food. I think one the reasons for the difference in how we react compared to children on the autism spectrum is because of our social understanding and communication skills. These help us to navigate through the social world by providing appropriate excuses, or enduring some experiences with the knowledge that they are only for a short duration. Difficulties in these areas make it particularly difficult for children on the autism spectrum to cope with sensory perception differences.

Theoretical basis

The fields of neurology, psychology and occupational therapy contribute to the knowledge of sensory perception differences. However, since these fields are discrete from each other, their beliefs regarding the causation and possible strategies are also varied. Researchers from a neurological perspective suggest that people with autism have structural abnormalities in the cerebellum area of their brains. As a result there is a disruption in the way the brain is able to pay attention or shift attention from one kind of source to another (Townsend et al. 1996). Perhaps this explains why some people with autism comment that they are able to either look at someone or listen to them but cannot do both things at the same time. Blairs and Slater (2007) comment that the sensory input impacts the arousal level of our brains and the required response for the input. When the arousal state is optimal we are able to function well, but when there is over-arousal it can lead to stress and anxiety in the individual. This heightened anxious state can lead to abnormal reactions or insistence on engaging in calming activities which may or may not be socially acceptable, such as flicking fingers in front of their eyes.

Ornitz (1974) shares this opinion and argues that the self-stimulatory behaviours seen in children with autism are caused by sensory perception difficulties. He suggests that since people with autism are unable to filter the irrelevant information (sometimes called gestalt perception) they often experience sensory overload. For example, when you walk into a shopping centre you do not necessarily pay attention to all the people, lights and smells there. You try to focus on the relevant information and ignore all the information that is not necessary. If you imagine that you are unable to do this, you can think how exhausting it can be to spend even 15 minutes in such a place. According to Ornitz (1974), children engage in self-stimulatory or repetitive behaviours so that they can cope with the information they are receiving from different sensations. He attributed the difference in sensory perception seen in people on the spectrum to the abnormal functioning of the brain stem. As babies grow, brain maturation takes place during which the brain learns to ignore the irrelevant information (Snyder et al. 2004). It appears that this process is not taking place in children with autism.

During the summer holidays Karen changed the colour of her hair. When she went back to work, Callum refused to work with her. Karen persisted in trying to engage him but without any success. She then considered whether the change of her hair colour had anything to do with Callum's behaviour and dyed her hair back to the normal shade. Callum immediately started working with her again!

A psychological theory which is sometimes used to explain the sensory differences in autism is the weak central coherence theory (Frith 1989). As we have already discussed in previous chapters, this theory suggests that people with autism tend to focus on parts of an object rather than perceiving the whole. On the basis of this, children with autism may show sensory abnormalities because, even though they may see or experience the whole thing, their processing styles allow them only to focus on a small portion, and this produces fragmented perceptions of the given information. In this case study, it is possible that Callum recognizes Karen only on the basis of her hair, and failed to recognize her with a different colour hair.

Plaisted et al. (1998) agreed with this view on the basis of their research on visual discrimination in people with autism. They suggested that people with autism have heightened discrimination skills, as a result of which they are good at identifying the uniqueness of various objects. However, this skill does not help them to see the commonalities between the objects. Therefore, a child may be able to differentiate between the cornflakes from different companies and insist on eating only those from specific brands.

Strategies to use

Sensory integration therapy (Ayres 1979) is an approach that is mainly used by occupational therapists to work with children who have sensory difficulties. This therapy is based on the philosophy that the child's brain has not matured properly and aims to provide the appropriate exercises and experiences to help this process. Thus an improved nervous system will lead to decrease in sensory dysfunction and the associated behaviours. This approach should only be followed by trained professionals as it is believed that providing an inappropriate level of stimulation will not be beneficial for the child; its effectiveness is still debatable. In their analysis of different studies conducted using sensory integration therapy, Lang et al. (2012) concluded that the evidence for its effectiveness is inconclusive.

In spite of this, this approach is gaining popularity and various studies have been conducted to observe its use in an educational setting. Schilling and Schwartz (2004) found that sitting children on a therapy ball in an early years setting improved their in-seat behaviour and increased their engagement in the activities. The study suggests that since the children could regulate their own movement it provided them with the appropriate vestibular and proprioceptive stimulation to maintain their level of arousal. Impressive as this study sounds, it is important to consider the impact of offering a ball to sit on to some children in the setting while others may not be allowed to have such an opportunity.

Weighted vests or wristbands are also being used by some professionals and practitioners to provide the child with proprioceptive feedback. It is believed that weighted vests can help with inattention and reduce repetitive behaviours. However, there is very little research into its impact on young children. Stephenson and Carter (2009) conducted an analysis of the existing studies on their use with children with autism and concluded that the evidence for their effectiveness is limited. Therefore, these should also be used under appropriate guidance from an occupational therapist.

It may start to feel that this knowledge is not necessarily contributing to any interventions that you can use. One of the first steps that you as a practitioner can take is being sensitive to the possibility of sensory perception difficulties for the child you are working with. Try to understand how a particular situation can feel to that child. You can be alert to the behaviours that the child is exhibiting to help you in this process. For example, if the child is closing his ears during playtime you may need to think of providing him with an acceptable alternative to cope with that situation, such as earphones or a different playtime. This is true for most children who are hypersensitive to a type of stimulation. It is also useful to evaluate your setting and how you can reduce the sensory overload being experienced by the child. You may think about covering floor surfaces, using rubber caps on table and chair legs, or not talking among yourselves when working with the child. While providing these changes, you also need to work on desensitizing the child to the sensation. This basically means introducing the child to the sensation in a graded fashion. In this case, the child may be exposed to the noise of three children in the playground. Once he is able to cope with this, increase the number of children slowly. Similarly, for children who are hyposensitive (or seek the sensation), provide them with appropriate forms of that stimulation. For example, if the child is jumping from the top of the furniture you could perhaps try providing some time on a trampoline so that he gets the required proprioception input. Or if a child is smearing his faeces you may want to introduce some messy play with more appropriate substances.

If the child is having difficulty in processing the information itself, it is important that the environment is simplified so that it is easier for him to process the required information. You may also need to highlight what is the relevant information which he needs to pay attention to. For example, teach the child that when the light switch is turned off it means the activity is finished, if you use such rules in your setting. Similarly, if the child is facing a sensory overload you need to think of offering him opportunities for some quiet time. This could be finding a quiet corner in the nursery, or giving him some sunglasses or a toy to squeeze. It is important to notice signs of sensory overload (usually when the child is not responding or is getting distressed) and provide the space before it turns into a 'challenging behaviour' situation. It would also be a good idea to teach the child to seek these breaks by giving him a sign or teaching the words 'I need a break' so that he is able to regulate his behaviour. Everyone's notions of enjoyable sensory experiences are different. The best way to know what the child you work with likes is to gather evidence by observing the child rather than going with your own preconceived notions.

Summary of the main points

- Most children with autism have difficulties in making sense of sensory information.
- Difficulties in sensory processing can lead to self-stimulatory behaviours as well as challenging behaviours.
- Adapting the setting or providing aids to reduce the sensory overload may be necessary for some children to function in the setting.
- Children may also need desensitizing programmes to enable them to cope with these sensations.
- Seeking the help of an occupational therapist can be beneficial in providing the child with appropriate sensory input.

> **Activity time**
>
> - Observe a child with autism and talk to his or her family members to identify what the child's sensory needs are.
> - Think of how the early years setting can be adapted to enable the child to function better in the setting.

Useful websites

Rompa: www.rompa.com/shop.html
Sensory warehouse: www.sensorytoywarehouse.com
Winslow: www.winslow-cat.com

Behaviour difficulties

Difficult or inappropriate behaviours are often associated with children with autism. The most common behaviours which are quoted are: difficulties in eating, sleeping and coping with changes; and engaging in stereotypical and ritualistic behaviours. In fact there is a lot of research around eating difficulties shown in these children. Schreck et al. (2004) conducted a comparative study of children with autism and typical children. They found that children with autism tolerated a more restricted range of foods and were more particular about following certain mealtime routines (such as wanting the same utensils). These children also more often refused certain foods because of their texture. As can be seen, behaviours considered as problems are often complex because they include a range of difficulties experienced by these children. One of the main things to remember is that behaviours do not happen in isolation. There is a reason for any behaviour to take place, which is usually the result of an interaction with others.

Communication difficulties

Difficulty in this area is a main characteristic of autism. As has been seen in the chapter on communication, children may have difficulties in both receptive and expressive communication. This would mean that they may not be able to express what their needs are, and may also not understand what is being communicated to them.

> Ryan's class went to the seaside during the summer for a day out. All the children were offered a choice of either having fish or hot-dogs and chips. When Ryan was asked whether he would like a hot-dog he started crying 'no dog please' and tried to run away from the restaurant.

Literal understanding of language as in this case can also lead to behaviour difficulties. Carr (1985) argued that the communicative function of behaviour should not be ignored when working with children with limited communication skills. A number of others have also shared this opinion and stated that the frequency of aggressive behaviour decreases as the person's communication abilities increase (Cheseldine and Stansfield 1993; Russell and Harris 1993). Commenting on the role of language, Vygotsky (1962) stated that not only does language help in concept formation, but internalized language helps children to reflect on their own behaviour and guide it to the desired goal. When children do not have this ability it will be more difficult for them to be in control of their own behaviour or to consider themselves to be responsible for it.

Difficulties in social understanding

Limited social understanding and difficulties in social interaction constitute another main feature of autism. Murphy et al. (2005) have pointed out that poor expressive language and social interaction skills can lead to inappropriate behaviours in people with autism and learning difficulties.

> Six-year-old Isobel is able to use the toilet appropriately in a familiar situation; however, she does not mind relieving herself at any location in an unfamiliar situation when she does not know where the toilet is or cannot find one.

Here, Isobel has understood the routine of using the toilet but does not understand the social significance of this behaviour. Therefore, not understanding the subtle social rules can also cause inappropriate behaviours.

However, the very nature of social interaction is that it involves other people. Since some children with autism can be aloof (Wing 1996) and not interact with their carers, it can be difficult for their family members or the practitioners to consistently engage with an unresponsive child. Sinason (1992) states that, as a result of this, people tend to reduce their interactions with the child over a period of time. This not only limits the opportunities for the child to learn the appropriate skills, but can also make him feel lonely if he does want to have company but does not know how to express this in an appropriate way – which can lead to an increase in inappropriate ways of interacting.

Flexible thinking and imagination

Difficulties in this area could arise for a number of reasons, such as lack of theory of mind (Baron-Cohen et al. 1985), weak central coherence (Frith 2003) and executive functioning difficulties (Ozonoff 1995). As discussed in other chapters, children with autism can find it difficult to understand others' emotions and intentions, and to predict possible outcomes. All of these can make the child extremely anxious and consequently perhaps reluctant to accept any changes, or he will establish his own routines and rituals. Hill (2004) suggests that the difficulties in planning caused by executive function difficulties could make following activities which need sequencing skills and self-monitoring difficult for these children. As a result the child may find daily activities such as eating or dressing difficult to do. It has been argued that insistence on an unchanging routine is one of the ways the child makes the world predictable and understandable.

Sensory perceptions

Steve likes to hear loud sounds and vibration and often keeps his ear right next to the computer speakers or the CD player. One day the crèche did not have any music playing as the CD player was broken; Steve gave the CD player a few shakes and tried to lead members of staff towards it. When none of these resulted in music being played, Steve got distressed and threw the CD player on the floor. Steve kept hitting his ear for the rest of the day.

As discussed in the previous chapter, Leekam et al. (2007) state that sensory abnormalities are more common in people on the autism spectrum. As a result of this, children may be hypersensitive, hyposensitive or have fluctuating responses to the various sensations (Bogdashina 2003). It has been suggested that some of the self-stimulatory behaviours seen in children could be because of these abnormalities (Delacato 1974). Insistence on wearing specific clothes or eating specific types of food can also be attributed to this (Plaisted et al. 1998). As seen in the above case study, a need for sensory stimulation, along with difficulties in communication and social understanding, can also lead to self-injurious or destructive behaviours.

Other causes

In addition to the above areas of specific difficulties, children with autism may have other medical conditions or disabilities which can contribute to certain behaviours. Children may also exhibit difficult behaviours when they are not motivated by an activity. It has been suggested that when the environment is not sufficiently stimulating, children may engage in self-stimulatory behaviour or resort to chal-lenging behaviour (Repp et al. 1988). It is important, therefore, to also pay attention to the relevance of the activities you do with the children in your setting and whether they are too difficult or too easy for the child.

Behaviour assessment and planning

It is clear from the above discussion that behaviour problems are often used by individuals to achieve their goals (Goldiamond

1974). To identify the cause of a behaviour, detailed observation of the nature, function and conditions that lead to or maintain the behaviour needs to be undertaken (O'Brien 1998). One way of assessing the behaviour is known as functional analysis. In a study conducted by Reese et al. (2005), where functional analysis was used to compare the reasons for the problem behaviours in children with and without autism, they found that children with autism usually indulged in these behaviours to access an item they wanted or to avoid unpleasant sensory stimulation. In comparison, children without autism used such behaviours to gain their caregiver's attention or to escape their demands. They also found that there were differences in the functions of the behaviours for boys with autism compared to girls. Studies such as these highlight that it is important to understand each individual child and his needs rather than making any generalized assumptions.

A better understanding of the behaviour can be gathered by interviewing the family members and your colleagues as well as observing the child. A basic functional analysis of behaviour tries to gather information about what happened before the behaviour – or the 'antecedent'. Detailed records of the actual behaviour are also analysed, as are the consequences of that behaviour: did the child get out of the situation, or receive what he wanted? One of the main principles of this process is that once the function of the behaviour has been identified, a more socially acceptable alternative is provided to the child. It is argued that if an alternative is not provided, a different behaviour which serves the same function will replace the eradicated one (Cheseldine and Stansfield 1993).

With our increasing understanding of the causes of behaviour, an ecological assessment of the behaviour is often conducted along with the functional analysis; this permits an evaluation of how the setting and the people in it might also be contributing towards the behaviour occurrence. Zarkowska and Clements (1994) introduced an assessment called the STAR approach. Here the setting, triggers, actions and results are all evaluated as shown in the table.

The information required for the behaviour assessment:

Setting	Triggers	Actions	Results
What was the physical climate of the setting like (noise, smell, movement in the room, temperature)? What kind of interaction style was being used (was the child being given any choice to express what he likes)? Were the activities provided appropriate for the child (in terms of their structure, their level of interest for the child, their level of challenge)? How was the child's general state of health (did he miss sleep or breakfast, was he feeling ill)? What was the emotional state of the child (was he anxious, has the family moved house, are his parents separating)?	Information about the context immediately before the behaviour happened; what you think may have triggered the behaviours (whether someone else came near the child, was there a change in activity, was the smell of food coming from the kitchen?).	Actions are the observable behaviour that takes place. You need to note information such as what the child did, and how long for.	What was the outcome of the actions? Did the child get what he wanted? Did the child manage to avoid what he do not want? Was the child punished for his behaviour? Was the child still asked to complete the given task?

One of the first steps when using the STAR approach is to agree on what actions are being observed. This means that you, along with your colleagues, will have to decide which behaviour you are observing and be precise in your description. Vague, non-specific terms such as 'temper tantrums' or 'a wobbly' should be avoided. Give an exact description of what happened, such as 'the child started crying and overturned the dinner plate'. When the actual behaviours have been identified, only then can alternative behaviours be established or strategies to manage them introduced.

Conducting a behaviour assessment is a difficult process. It is also possible that sometimes you may not know all the relevant information or not realize the significance of that information for the child.

Good communication between the family and the setting and among all the professionals involved with the child is vital to enable this process. You may also need to establish channels of communication which will help you to share this information amongst yourselves. For example, could the parent send a text message to let a staff member know that the child did not sleep in the night, so that the setting is ready for the child and activities can be planned accordingly? Remember also that the child may well exhibit the same behaviour to serve various functions. Therefore strategies will have to be developed accordingly and a clear way of evaluating whether they are working or not needs to be established. As this is a complex process you, along with your colleagues, will need to identify the behaviour you want to focus on. It is unrealistic to aim to change every behaviour you consider inappropriate, and this could be very frustrating for the child as well.

Possible strategies

If we take an ecological approach to behaviour where we do not consider the child to be solely responsible for all his behaviour, but acknowledge that the setting and others also contribute to it, then the strategies cannot be aimed at changing the child's behaviour only. Traditionally, early years settings tend to use rewards and punishments as the methods to manage behaviour. While these behaviourist strategies can be used as an interim measure, it is vital that the child is also taught appropriate alternative behaviours in the long term. The purpose of the short-term strategies is mainly to prevent the behaviour from happening or to defuse the behaviour when it does take place.

Short-term strategies

Once you have identified how the setting is contributing to the behaviour, it is possible to modify the setting to reduce the likelihood of the behaviour recurring. For example, if the child showed distress because he missed his breakfast, perhaps you could provide a light snack once he reaches the early years setting. Similarly, if the behaviour is happening because of the sensory overload in the setting then you need to consider how this stimulation can be reduced, or increased to engage the child. For example, could the particular staff member whose perfume seems to trigger the behaviour stop wearing that perfume? The content of the activity or the nature of the activity itself may have to be changed to keep it motivating for the child. Knowing about what motivates the child and what are his particular interests can help in this process. For example, a child I used to work with was fascinated by the moon and stars and I used these to teach numbers, different concepts such as big and small, and also as motivators for behaviour management.

If the behaviour is happening because of difficulties in communication and understanding social rules, try and make these as explicit as you can in your setting. Make good use of visual means by representing key information pictorially, if required. Try not to have a picture for every word as this can be meaningless for the child and also overwhelming. Hodgdon (1995) provides some very useful strategies for how visual information can be used to enable a person with autism to understand the expectations and prepare them for change. Pay particular attention to your communication style as well. Potter and Whittaker (2000) have provided some pointers of how staff might modify their approach and communication when working with children with autism to reduce the likelihood of inappropriate behaviour.

Along with these, strategies based on positive reinforcements can also be used to quickly manage the behaviour for a short duration. When using rewards with the child, make sure that you have a selection of rewards which are individualized for them, to be effective. If the child is provided with the same reward every day the novelty of the reward wanes, and he will soon stop responding to it. It is also crucial that you have a hierarchy of rewards so that you can match them to the nature of the task. For example, you can use a highly motivating reward for a task that the child finds particularly difficult to do. It is also important that the child understands this sequence of activities. Using a visual timetable based on TEACCH principles can help in this process. It may also be that the child will need a favoured activity before and after a particularly challenging task. Carr et al. (1976) found that embedding activities in this way can reduce the occurrence of inappropriate behaviour during teaching time.

This kind of behaviour contract can be followed with an immediate or a delayed reward. For example, if the child is able to cope with playing in the same room as another child, he will get to spend some time on a video game when he goes home. Having links like this between home and the setting can help to establish consistency in the approach. However, this delayed process will only work if the child is able to control his behaviour and has the prerequisite skills, such as waiting and the concept of time. A more accessible version is called 'token economy', where the child is given a token or sticker every time he shows the expected behaviour. A number of early years settings use these sticker chart-based systems. The point to remember when using them with children with autism is that the stickers or tokens have to be meaningful for the child to engage in the behaviour. Again, it might be important to visually represent what the relevance of the tokens is, such as showing that three tokens will lead to water play. For some children it may be necessary to make this more concrete by actually turning the photograph of the water play area into a jigsaw puzzle and teaching them that once the puzzle is complete they can go to play in the area.

One of the other behaviourist strategies which can be used effectively with some children is providing them with an incompatible behaviour. For example, if the child continuously pinches himself, giving him a small object to hold when he is not using his hands (such as at story times) will help stop this behaviour from occurring.

Punishments are usually ineffective for children with autism as they may not understand that they are being punished because of their behaviour. Therefore having a naughty chair or time out are not effective for the purpose they are used. However, some children with autism may need some time to relax or calm themselves when they find the given situation overwhelming.

Within the short-term strategies you also need to consider what your reaction will be if the behaviour happens in spite of the measures you take to avoid it. It is particularly important to have a behaviour policy in your setting so that everyone is using a consistent and agreed approach. Try to use a distraction technique such as tickling the child to attract their attention as a first step. You could also redirect the child to another activity in a calm manner. If the child is being physically aggressive, try to provide him with plenty of space and safeguard the other children. Use of physical restraint is usually not very effective in the long run and can be an unpleasant experience for everyone involved. It is also necessary that if such behaviour does take place, you discuss the situation with a colleague immediately after the incident so that you do not carry any negative feelings.

Long-term strategies

While short-term strategies can be used for a small amount of time, the ultimate aim should always be to teach the child to cope with the situation in a more appropriate manner. In fact, when a behaviour plan is drafted for the child it is good practice to identify the short-term as well as the long-term strategies. Having these in a written form will also help in having consistency among the different staff members.

You could use a range of strategies that have been discussed in this book to develop these skills. To develop communication skills and expand ritualized behaviour you could use an Intensive Interaction approach. Byers (1996) suggests that having such approaches also gives the individual an opportunity to control their environment. Picture Exchange Communication System (PECS) can be used to develop some initial requesting skills in the child. Using Bandura's (1969) social learning theory, modelling can teach social skills and rules. However, unless the individual understands why they are doing it, generalization of the skill learnt in this way will be limited. Social stories can help the child to understand the purpose of following these rules or behaviour. Crozier and Tincani (2007) found using social stories helped in reducing the inappropriate behaviours in some children. Similarly, understanding their own and others' emotions can be taught using some of the strategies discussed in this book. Flexibility can be developed by presenting change in a graded fashion. Fears and phobias or hypersensitivity to sensory stimulation can be reduced by systematic desensitization (Wolpe 1958). Zarkowska and Clements (1994) also suggest providing relaxation techniques. With small children this usually will have to be conditioned, so that for example a specific piece of music or smell is used when the child is happy and relaxed, and after repeated exposures the child will slowly start associating this experience with being relaxed. Once this has happened it can be used as a defusing technique or offered to the child as an option he can use in a stressful situation. The focus of any behaviour intervention should always be the well-being of the child and providing him with a sense of ownership for his behaviour.

Worked-out case study

Ryan's key worker Rashida is finding it difficult to get him to eat any food. While discussing it with his mother, she finds out that Ryan only eats plain pasta at home when it is warm. Rashida did not realize this and has been putting ketchup on his pasta some days to make it more appealing for him. Ryan's mother also informed her that he only eats when fed and often walks around the house while eating.

Behaviour difficulties:
- Not eating
- Not sitting at the table

Possible reasons for the behaviour:
- Ryan has sensory perception difficulties and does not like food of any different colour, and needs it at a specific temperature.
- He may also have poor body awareness and cannot hold cutlery.
- Ryan may have difficulties in motor-planning and finds holding and using cutlery difficult.
- He does not understand the social rules about eating at a table.
- He is finding it difficult to cope with change in the setting and the people feeding him.

Strengths and likes:
- Is very good at matching
- Likes Thomas the Tank Engine
- Likes to play on the swing

Possible short-term strategies:
- Warm the food and feed him.
- Use a visual timetable to show that after eating he can play on a swing.
- Allow him to hold a Thomas toy if he sits at the table while eating.
- Refer to an occupational therapist.

Possible long-term strategies:
- Slowly desensitize him to eating food at different temperatures. For example, allow him to try a small amount of pasta before eating the warm pasta.
- Introduce different foods in a similar manner (start with other foods which are white in colour, such as rice or bread). Initially let him cope with having the food on the table, then slowly touch and then taste.
- Provide a range of motor-skill activities to develop his grip.
- Use a visual timetable to introduce changes.
- Teach about the mealtime rules at the setting.

Summary of the main points

- Inappropriate behaviours usually occur for a reason. It is important to identify the cause of the behaviour before any intervention is planned.
- Behaviour assessment should involve all the relevant people and include a range of settings to get a comprehensive picture.
- It is important to have short-term strategies which provide immediate results and help in managing behaviour. However, the long-term strategy should always provide the child with the necessary skills to manage his behaviour.
- Consistency is important for the strategies to be effective. Having a written behaviour intervention plan will help in this process.

Activity time

- Make a list of some of the behaviours that you consider difficult for a child you work with. Ask a colleague to make a list of their own as well. Compare the lists and think how you will identify a behaviour that you both want to focus on.
- Conduct a behaviour assessment for a child using the STAR approach and identify what contributes to the behaviour.
- Think about how the setting and the activities can be manipulated to reduce the behaviour happening.

Useful websites

Challenging Behaviour Foundation: www.challengingbehaviour.org.uk
National Autistic Society: www.nas.org.uk

9

Working with other professionals

It is estimated that a child with autism will be in contact with approximately five to eight professionals during their childhood. These could be professionals coming from a range of backgrounds such as teachers, learning support assistants, early years support teams, autism advisors, educational psychologists, nursery nurses, speech and language therapists, occupational therapists, health visitors and paediatricians. This seems to be the case whether or not the child is attending a specialist or a mainstream setting. This would mean that as an early years practitioner working with a child on the spectrum you are likely to engage with professionals from the various disciplines. There is also an increasing legal expectation that professionals should work together. This chapter discusses the rationale for this and the issues that can arise in such joint work, and finally provides some ideas for dealing with these issues.

David is a bit confused as to what his approach with Radhika should be. The speech and language therapist who came to see her suggested that he should insist that Radhika gives him eye contact before giving her anything she requests. This was agreed and has been set as a target for her. However, the autism advisor specified that some people with autism find it difficult to give eye contact and he should not force her to do so. She suggested that David should be concentrating on developing a meaningful communication system for Radhika.

This is a common experience for practitioners in early years, which illustrates the need for professionals to work together. As each professional brings their own expertise and knowledge, working together can help in reducing duplication and providing cohesive support to the child and the family (and you). Joint planning could provide the child with fewer achievable targets rather than each specialist setting their own discrete ones as in the above case. Sharing information among professionals can lead to development of their skills. It is also likely that when professionals from the various fields come together they will have a better idea of the full set of issues and strengths that the child has. This can encourage them to see the child as a complete person rather than focusing only on the specific difficulties in their area of work. Parents in the study conducted by Hodge and Runswick-Cole (2008) stated that they appreciate it when the professionals treat their child in this way. There is also an argument that by sharing knowledge and working together the professionals could save money as there is less duplication of services.

It is clear, then, that working together as a team has many benefits for the child as well as for the professionals. However, just as there are different models of parent participation, as discussed in Chapter 3, there are also different levels of engagement among the professionals. Orelove and Sobsey (1991) define some of the terms which are used to describe joint working. They state that the term 'multidisciplinary' is used to explain that the professionals from various fields are working alongside each other. However, this does not necessarily lead to shared resources, and each focuses on their area of specialism only. The speech and language therapist and the autism advisor in the above case study seem to be following this approach.

Orelove and Sobsey (1991) suggest that the next level of joint working is called 'interdisciplinary'. Here the professionals are involved in actively sharing information, and often generate plans and programmes together. Although the negotiation and planning process takes place as a team, it is expected that each professional has their own area of expertise and hence is responsible for implementing the programme which relates to their area. Building on the above case study, the speech therapist and autism advisor could have jointly assessed Radhika and agreed on a strategy to follow for developing her communication skills. Then the speech and language therapist could have focused on implementing the communication aspect, and the autism advisor could have helped the setting in making the communication and language skills required for the curriculum accessible for the student.

The third model of working that Orelove and Sobsey explain is the 'transdisciplinary' approach. Here professionals are not only engaged in planning interventions, but share information and engage in transferring their skills to each other. In this model, the professional boundaries are blurred, which enables a variety of professionals to provide effective support to the child. These professionals may still contact the experts for specific input as and when required. For example, the autism advisor may conduct the assessment of Radhika's communication skills on her own and devise a plan, but contact the speech and language therapist for any specialist input required. The idea of children's centres in England, where teams of professionals are co-located, working as a joint team, and professionals from different fields are managed by one manager, is based on this model.

Depending on the kind of early years setting you are working in, you may have experience of one or more of these types of joint working. The aspiration is to move towards interdisciplinary or transdisciplinary approaches. However, just like different models of partnership working with parents, it may be necessary to have a more flexible approach in working with professionals as well.

Issues in joint working

Looking at these various models also highlights why it can be difficult to work in collaboration with each other. It is possible that when professionals from different organizations or fields come together they are apprehensive about the structure of a different setting, in terms of the hierarchy in the place and what is the acceptable code of practice. Professionals may also have different legislations which dictate what they are allowed to disclose and discuss. For example, the directions of patient confidentiality are more stringent in the medical profession, and people working in this field, such as a speech and language therapist or a health visitor, may be reluctant to share the complete information they have about the child or the family with the early years practitioner.

It is true that each profession approaches a child with autism and his family from its own theoretical position and therefore when professionals from these fields are working together what they expect as an appropriate approach could be different. For example, the focus for the social worker could be child protection issues whereas a portage worker may be interested in developing the child's skills and parental confidence in working with their child. For these two professionals to work effectively together, they need to have a shared understanding of the focus of their work. On the other hand, to work in a transdisciplinary approach it is imperative that the professional boundaries are blurred. Some professionals may fear that their identity will be lost in this process (Robinson and Cottrell 2005). Professionals may view themselves in a hierarchical way and consider that their opinions or strategies are less or more important than others'. This can hinder the process of joint working as they may be less willing to negotiate. Even when the professionals want to work together they may not have sufficient training or guidance about how to work in this way (Anning and Edwards 1999).

On a practical level, working together in an interdisciplinary or transdisciplinary model would require professionals to spend a considerable amount of time with each other to discuss, plan and learn from each other. This may not always be possible when professionals are working with huge caseloads. Professionals from different fields are likely to use different terminology, where the same word can mean different things or the same thing can be expressed in different ways. For example, some medical professionals may still use terms such as mental retardation and classify different levels of mental retardation in children. By contrast, in the education sector in the UK the commonly used term is learning difficulties, and more and more professionals in this field are moving away from classifying the ability of the child on the basis of intelligence tests. This said, not all professionals may feel confident to request a clarification of the terminology, either because of where they see themselves on the hierarchy of professions, or because they do not want to appear ignorant or as though they are trying to be awkward. This feeling of being judged can also impact on other interactions, for example where the early years practitioner may feel threatened by the autism advisor observing them, because they may feel that their practice is being evaluated.

Good practice guidelines

Considering all these issues, it would appear as if joint working with other professionals could be an impossible task to achieve. I would argue that although it can be challenging to work in this fashion it is not unachievable. It is necessary that every effort is made to establish and sustain a positive working relationship with all the different professionals for the benefit of the child. A lot of this is dependent on the ethos of the setting and the message that is given to the staff as well as the external professionals. It is often important in an early years setting for someone to have the role of coordinating the interactions with the external agencies or interdisciplinary teams, such as the special needs coordinators in the UK. Having one point of contact can make it easier for both internal and external professionals to know who to contact in the setting.

It is vital that the setting clarifies the roles and responsibilities of the different professionals so that no one feels threatened, and also to avoid overlap of roles. This information should not only be shared at a managerial level but among the practitioners too, and sadly this is not always the case. For instance, when I was working as an advisory teacher for autism and visiting a large early years setting, a learning support assistant for one of the children I was working with assumed that I was the speech and language therapist, while another support worker in a different class thought I was an educational psychologist! The management and the teachers in this setting were clearly not communicating with the learning support assistants. The onus was also on me as an external professional to make sure that the people I was working with at least understood the nature of my role. Although this should happen as standard practice, you may find that as a practitioner you sometimes have to take the initiative to find out such information. This process of clarification could also help in dispelling any wrong ideas that different people may have, such as a teacher feeling she is being judged by the advisor.

Effective joint working requires everyone to have respect for each other, and understanding that every individual makes an important contribution in the process of helping the child. Such values need to be shared among the whole team. Dale (1996) suggests that there should be assigned time for the team to air their concerns and plan together. This would allow them to share information and discuss the viewpoints from the different professional angles and help to build a comprehensive picture of the child. However, for this to be effective all professionals should feel that their views are considered as important and that there is no hierarchy. It is useful also if common vocabulary is shared as far as possible. Along with this, have an open interaction so that even if some professional uses field-specific terminology, the person who could not understand the vocabulary or the process should feel confident to be able to ask for clarification. If this is not happening, the chair of the meeting can always ask the professional to simplify or rephrase the comment. When such behaviour is modelled by senior members of staff it will provide confidence to others in seeking clarifications.

It is ideal to have these case discussions face to face, but as discussed earlier lack of time is one of the main concerns for a number of professionals. Therefore, viable alternatives should be tried wherever possible, whether this includes a conference phone call, discussing via email or using Skype. Systems which are not solely dependent on written communication will also engage staff members or parents who are more comfortable in using speech. In addition, avoiding travelling to a meeting can be time-saving.

It is expected that family members will be included in these discussions to ensure that there is successful collaboration between the early years setting and home. Where it is necessary to have a meeting without the family members, or the family members are unable to attend a meeting, you need to have procedures in place for sharing information about the family with the other professionals to maintain their confidentiality (Dale 1996). It is possible that a family member may have shared information with you at a personal level with no thought that this would be shared with your colleagues or with other professionals. The setting or the practitioner needs to clarify to the family that this is likely to happen and seek their permission before sharing information with anyone else.

As some of the issues for successful joint working are related to people having different theoretical backgrounds and discrete specialisms, joint training has often been suggested as a way of developing interprofessional working (D'Amour and Oandasan 2005).

Ideally this takes place during the initial training period itself. Whether or not this is the case, it is useful to have these opportunities on an ongoing basis. Again, depending on your setting you may be able to have access to training programmes run at a local authority level which professionals from different backgrounds can attend. Even if you are in a smaller establishment you could explore creative ideas of how joint training or knowledge-sharing can take place. This may, for example, be part of your staff meetings, where you either invite other professionals to share their expertise or involve them when you are discussing a relevant area. For instance, you could request the speech and language therapist to provide some ideas for encouraging communication in children with autism. At other times you could invite them when you are discussing the early years curriculum with regard to language and communication. Having this knowledge will enable them to support you in a way that will help in meeting the statutory requirements for the child. According to Molyneux (2001), having creative working methods is an indicator of positive joint working in an interprofessional team.

Processes and procedures can only go so far in addressing the issues. The other factor which contributes to this process is the personal attributes of the practitioner. Barnes (2008) provides a number of these which she thinks are required. For joint working to be successful, there needs to be commitment at an individual level to work in this way. This would require the individual to have good social-communication skills, willing to listen to the other person and able to view the situation from their perspective. As it is unlikely that two people coming from different positions will always agree, the practitioner also needs to be flexible and to be able to negotiate. Sometimes this can lead to prioritizing different skills or strategies from those you want to focus on. As not every professional is able to work in this way, you will also need some persistence to continue engaging them. Finally, you need to be able to research and find out about local professionals and their roles so that you can network with them as and when required. Successful joint working emerges from this desire to work with others to solve difficulties faced by the child or their family while also engaging them in this process as contributors and decision-makers.

Summary of the main points

- Working with other professionals is an essential part of the early years practitioner's role and often a legal requirement.
- There are a number of benefits for working in this way, such as providing achievable targets and getting a comprehensive picture of the child's life.
- However, effective joint working is a complicated process and there could be a number of issues in organizing this – for instance, time, different knowledge bases and different priorities.
- Having clear agreed values and aims can help in working as a team. Clear understanding of roles and responsibilities, respect for each other and a personal commitment are the other factors which can help in making this work.

Activity time

- Find out about the different professionals involved with the child you are working with. Research into their roles if you are not aware of them.
- Reflect on your own strengths and areas for development in relation to joint working skills. How could you improve your ways of working with the other professionals?
- Evaluate the strategies which are used in your setting to encourage joint working. What amendments can be made to these to make your practice even better?

Useful website

Inclusion Development Programme early years guide: www.education.gov.uk/publications/standard/publicationDetail/Page1/DCSF-00040-2009

10 Moving to primary school

Moving from an early years setting to a primary school can be difficult for most children but especially challenging for those on the autism spectrum because of their difficulties in communication, social understanding and coping with change. Some children on the spectrum may also find the increase in sensory input in a bigger school distressing. This process is not only a cause of concern for children, but also for their parents. Gray (2003) has shown that finding an appropriate school placement is one of the main causes of parental stress. An early years practitioner can make this process easier by supporting the child and his family. This chapter discusses some of the key things to consider when supporting the family in making decisions about the school placement, as well as preparing the child for the change.

It is very likely that the family members may seek your opinion about what you consider to be the best placement for their child. Although there is a range of possible schooling options, there is little research evidence to suggest that any one type of setting is better for children on the autism spectrum compared to the other. Therefore most families and professionals make decisions on the basis of their own perceptions and instincts. The decision factors include the parents' and professionals' belief as to whether or not inclusion is appropriate for children on the spectrum. This may also be influenced by what they consider to be the child's needs and strengths and the level of support that they think the child should receive. Finally, it is also dependent on what is available locally and what the policy of the local authority is in relation to inclusion and special educational needs.

Even so, there is a possible range of school options from which the family has to choose. Over the years there has been a strong emphasis in the UK on inclusion of children with autism in mainstream schools. There is legislation in place which supports the child and his family in choosing a mainstream school if that is what the family wants. The strengths of such a school are that it will be local, which would mean that the child will have an opportunity to build on the friendships made in the school. If they have siblings, then it is possible that they would be going to the same school, which can be convenient for the family for making childcare arrangements. It is possible that the child may get additional support in the school. The main disadvantage of such a placement is that the teaching staff may not have any specific training in working with children on the autism spectrum. A mainstream school with a resource base for autism is another possibility. The staff in these units tend to have some training or experience of working with children with autism. The amount of time that the child spends in the resource base and the mainstream schoolrooms varies, depending on the school ethos. If run properly, these can provide the benefits of a mainstream placement along with specialist support.

Some families may feel that they would like their child to go to a special school. This could be a school for a range of special educational needs or specific to children with autism. It is likely (although not statutory) that teachers in such settings may have some training in autism. These schools also tend to have specialist support such as speech therapy, occupational therapy and music therapy in place. The number of children per class is small, with most having no more than ten children. However, although the overall staff–student ratio is higher, children may not necessarily get individual support. Sometimes such schools may not be available locally and may either involve a long time spent on travelling, or considering a residential placement. If the school is not local, then it can impact on family life and the child's social networks.

A small percentage of parents may also consider home schooling their child. This is mainly the case when the family wants to follow a specific intervention programme such as those based on applied behaviour analysis (ABA) or the Options approach. Both of these expect intensive, individual input for the child. These programmes claim excellent results for the child and take away all the difficulties that a school setting will pose for a child with autism. However, research evidence for the efficacy of either of these programmes is limited. They also require a lot of time and commitment from the family, which can influence their family life. Accessing funding for such programmes is another main concern. In their study of the experiences of parents who were following a home school programme based on ABA, Dillenburger et al. (2010) found that none of the parents were given money to cover full-time home schooling. In some local authorities, other services such as speech and language therapist support may be withdrawn if the child is funded for the home school programme.

Choosing a school

As this suggests, there is no ideal school for all children on the spectrum, and each option has its strengths and limitations. The choice has to be made on the basis of individual circumstances and beliefs. Irrespective of the type of school that the family chooses, there are certain general guidelines which need to be considered. When visiting a school, it is important to find out the staff expertise and knowledge in autism. This may not necessarily require them to have specific training, but could be based on their experience of working with children with autism. It is worth observing the interaction between the staff and children as this may give an idea of the school ethos and how approachable the staff are in general.

It is useful to know what the school's educational approach is to working with pupils with autism. Encourage the family to make a note of any evidence of this when they go to see the school. For example, do they see visual timetables being used, are the children using a range of communication means, are there opportunities for the child to learn in a distraction-free environment if that is required? This kind of information will also provide an insight into whether the school tends to focus on the deficits of the child only, or whether they balance this with developing the child's strengths too. Research evidence for the various approaches developed for working with children on the autism spectrum shows that none of them work for all children or cover all areas of learning. It is generally useful if the staff members are aware of a range of approaches and strategies, which they use according to individual requirements. The physical and human resources available to the school are another important consideration.

Research evidence suggests that children with autism benefit from having opportunities to interact with typically developing children (Kohler et al. 2007), so it is worth finding out if and how often this happens. Again, just like observing the staff interaction, it is useful to observe the peer interactions with existing pupils with disabilities. It is more likely that children with autism will experience rejection by their peers due to their social difficulties (Odom et al. 2006), therefore a strong inclusive ethos is necessary. Suggest to the child's parents that they request the school's behaviour policy or ask how bullying is dealt with. The final important consideration could be how the school involves and communicates with the family. The level of interaction that each family expects from the school is different, and getting this information beforehand will enable them to decide if they are satisfied with the involvement offered.

It is possible that some of the parents you work with are proactive and are aware of how autism impacts their child, what services are available locally and how to access them. In fact, Woodgate et al. (2008) have found that this was more often the case with parents who have children on the autism spectrum compared to those with other disabilities. However, not all parents share similar personalities or have the same resources. The level of support that the family will require has to be assessed on an individual basis. If you are working with a family who have recently immigrated to the country, they may need more help in understanding the processes and available services. One of the nurseries that I used to visit had a situation where a child whose parents had recently immigrated to the UK had no school placement for about seven months as the parents were not aware how early they needed to apply for a place. Having an opportunity to discuss the transition process well in advance with the family can avoid such circumstances.

Preparing for transition

Moving to the new school involves a number of changes for the child. As has been discussed in this book, children with autism find it easier to cope with changes if they are prepared for them. Once the family has selected the school and the child has been offered a place, make contact with the school. Quintero and McIntyre (2011) have found that teachers in mainstream primary schools are generally more concerned about a new child with autism starting in their class than a pupil with any other disability. Lack of collaboration between the early years setting and the primary school was cited as one of the reasons for the difficulties in transitions that children face. This can be reduced if the school staff are included in the transition planning meeting. This will provide an opportunity for your setting, the family, staff from the new school and any other external professionals involved to meet together to share concerns and strategies and plan a smooth transition. It is likely that, along with the change of setting, some of the external professionals and services may also change when the child moves to the new school. This information needs to be shared with the family and the school along with the contact details of the continuing professionals.

Having a 'communication passport' which includes information that is relevant and pertinent for the child will help the new setting. This can include information such as what the child likes or dislikes, how he communicates, what triggers his behaviour and things that the child is concerned about. Wherever possible, involve the child in developing this and personalize it so that he feels a sense of ownership. This can be supported with additional information about strategies that you have found useful. It is worth thinking about how your setting helped the child to settle when starting with you and passing on those hints to the school. Bringing these reflections to the meeting can help in generating newer ideas too, as group planning is generally more effective for this purpose (Zarkowska and Clements 1994).

You can also prepare children for the move by organizing some visits to the new school. To avoid sensory overload or other anxiety, it is sometimes preferred to arrange such visits when the school is empty; while this can be helpful in introducing them to the new setting, it is also important for them to see the school and the class as it would be functioning on a regular day. If this has not been organized, they may get distressed when they realize on their first day that they will have to share the school and the class with other children! Similarly, introduce them to the different locations in the school such as the playground and dining room. It would be easier for them to cope with these changes if they are accompanied by a familiar person from the early years setting. However, it is also necessary that the child gets to meet the new members of staff, where possible. This will also provide an opportunity for the new staff and staff from your setting to share key information.

It is crucial that the transition process is explained to the child. You could use visual supports such as having a timetable to explain when the change is going to take place (Hodgdon 1995). A transition book can also be prepared which explains to the child what is going to change in the new school and what will remain the same. This could be a small book which includes photographs of the new school, classroom, teaching staff and so on. If the child has this information during the holidays it can help in reducing his anxiety before the move and provide him with all the information he needs to understand. I have known some schools which have made a small video of their setting to share with the child, which is another excellent way of information sharing. Social stories (Gray 2000) can also be used for this purpose. You could also suggest to the family to have a few walks to the new school during the holidays so that the child gets familiar with the route.

If possible, contact the new school in the first week to find out if the child has settled or whether there is any further information which is required. It is important to remember that these are all only guidelines and you will need to individualize the process on the basis of the child, the family and the school's needs. With appropriate preparation it is possible to facilitate a smooth move to the primary school for the child. When a child you have worked with for a long time moves it can be a difficult time for you as well. However, the experiences you have had with the child and the knowledge you have gathered over the years will help you in supporting other children on the autism spectrum.

Summary of the main points

- Moving from one setting to another can be particularly stressful for a child on the autism spectrum, his family and the school staff.
- Some parents may need support when considering a schooling option for their child. As no single type of school can meet the needs of all children on the autism spectrum, this decision would have to be made on the basis of a range of factors.
- Providing the family with information about various settings and specific features that they need to look for can help them in the process of choosing a school.
- It is important that transition is well thought through and all the relevant people are involved in this process.
- Prepare the child for the move by providing them with all the necessary information.

Activity time

- Find out about the various types of schools which are available in your local area.
- Consider what will be the key information that you will need to pass on to a new member of staff who will be working with the child.
- Develop a communication passport and/or a transition booklet for the child based on one of the templates from the web links in 'Useful websites'.

Useful websites

Communication passports: www.communicationpassports.org.uk
Norfolk's transition good practice guide: www.schools.norfolk.gov.uk/pupil-needs/autistic-spectrum-disorder-asd/ncco97041

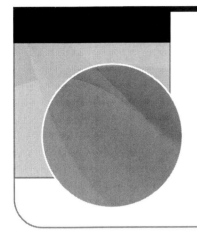

Note on vocabulary

Autism spectrum: I have mainly used autism or autism spectrum rather than the various subcategories. This book is relevant to anyone working with young children on the autism spectrum, irrespective of the label that they have been given.

Early years setting: I have used this phrase to represent any kind of provision working with young children, such as a crèche, playgroup or a nursery. Although children are considered to be in early years until the age of 8 years, the focus of this book is mainly up to the age of 5. However, practitioners working with some older children may also find the ideas suggested in the book useful.

Early years professional or practitioner: These terms have been used interchangeably to represent any person working with children in an early years setting.

He: Although there is some discussion in the field of autism about the prevalence rates of the condition based on gender, for now it is considered that autism is more common in boys than girls. Therefore, I have decided to use the pronoun 'he' when describing the child rather than the grammatically incorrect 'they'. It should be remembered, however, that this does not mean that this book is not oriented towards girls on the autism spectrum.

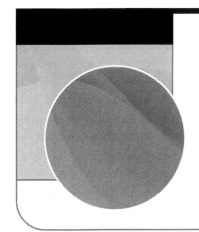

Reference list and further reading

Abbeduto, L., Seltzer, M. M., Shattuck, P., Krauss, M. W., Orsmond, G. and Murphy, M. M. (2004) Psychological well-being and coping in mothers of youths with autism, Down syndrome, or fragile X syndrome, *American Journal on Mental Retardation*, 109(3): 237–54.

Abraham, B. S. and Geschwind, D. H. (2008) Advances in autism genetics: on the threshold of a new neurobiology, *Nature Reviews Genetics*, 9(5): 341–55.

American Psychiatric Association (APA) (2000) *Diagnostic Statistical Manual of Mental Health Disorders*, 4th edn (text revised). Washington: APA.

Anning, A. and Edwards, A. (1999) *Promoting Children's Learning from Birth to Five: Developing the New Early Years' Professional*. Buckingham: Open University Press.

Ashwin, C., Baron-Cohen, S., Wheelwright, S., O'Riordan, M. and Bullmore, E. T. (2007) Differential activation of the amygdala and the 'social brain' during fearful face-processing in Asperger Syndrome, *Neurophysicologia*, 45(1): 2–14.

Attwood, T., Grandin, T., Bolick, T., Faherty, C., Iland, L., McIlwee Myers, J., Snyder, R., Wagner, S. and Wrobel, M. (2006) *Asperger's and Girls*. Arlington, TX: Future Horizons.

Ayres, A. J. (1979) *Sensory Integration and the Child*. Los Angeles: Western Psychological Services.

Bailey, T., Le Couteur, A., Gottesman, I., Bolton, P., Simonoff, E., Yuzda, E. and Rutter, M. (1995) Autism as a strongly genetic disorder: evidence from a British twin study, *Psychological Medicine*, 25(1): 63–77.

Baird, G., Simonoff, E., Pickles, A., Chandler, S., Loucas, T., Meldrum, D. and Charman, T. (2006) Prevalence of disorders of the autistic spectrum in a population cohort of children in South Thames: the Special Needs and Autism Project (SNAP), *The Lancet*, 368(9531): 210–15.

Bandura, A. (1969) *Principles of Behaviour Modification*. New York: Holt, Rinehart and Winston.

Barnes, P. (2008) Multi-agency working: what are the perspectives of SENCos and parents regarding its development and implementation?, *British Journal of Special Education*, 35(4): 230–40.

Baron-Cohen, S. (1987) Autism and symbolic play, *British Journal of Developmental Psychology*, 5(2): 139–48.

Baron-Cohen, S. (2004) *Mind Reading: Emotions Library*. London: Jessica Kingsley.

Baron-Cohen, S., Cox, A., Baird, G., Swettenham, J., Nightingale, N., Morgan, K., Drew, A. and Charman, T. (1996) Psychological markers in the detection of autism in infancy in a large population, *British Journal of Psychiatry*, 168(2): 158–63.

Baron-Cohen, S., Leslie, A. M. and Frith, U. (1985) Does the autistic child have a 'theory of mind'? *Cognition*, 21(1): 37–46.

Baron-Cohen, S., Scott, F. J., Allison, C., Williams, J., Bolton, P., Matthews, F. E. and Brayne, C. (2009) Prevalence of autism-spectrum conditions: UK school-based population study, *British Journal of Psychiatry*, 194(6): 500–9.

Bauminger, N., Shulman, C. and Agam, G. (2003) Peer interaction and loneliness in high-functioning children with autism, *Journal of Autism and Developmental Disorders*, 33(5): 489–507.

Bayat, M. (2007) Evidence of resilience in families of children with autism, *Journal of Intellectual Disability Research*, 5(9): 702–14.

Bettelheim, B. (1967) *Empty Fortress: Infantile Autism and the Birth of Self*. New York: Free Press.

Bishop, D. V. M. (1993) Autism, executive functions and theory of mind: a neuropsychological perspective, *Journal of Child Psychology and Psychiatry*, 34(3): 279–93.

Bishop, D. V. M., Whitehouse, A. J., Watt, H. J. and Line, E. A. (2008) Autism and diagnostic substitution: evidence from a study of adults with a history of developmental language disorder, *Developmental Medicine and Child Neurology*, 50(5): 341–5.

Blairs, S. and Slater, S. (2007) The clinical application of deep touch pressure with a man with autism presenting with severe anxiety and challenging behaviour, *British Journal of Learning Disabilities*, 35(4): 214–20.

Blake, R., Turner, L. M., Smoski, M. J., Pozdol, S. L. and Stone, W. L. (2003) Visual recognition of biological motion is impaired in children with autism, *Psychological Science*, 14(2): 151–7.

Bogdashina, O. (2003) *Sensory Perceptual Issues in Autism and Asperger Syndrome*. London: Jessica Kingsley.

Bondy, A. and Frost, L. (1994) The Delaware autistic program, in S. I. Harris and J. S. Handleman (eds) *Preschool Education Programs for Children with Autism*. Austin, TX: Pro-Ed.

Boudreau, E. and D'Entremont, B. (2010) Improving the pretend play skills of pre-schoolers with autism spectrum disorders: the effects of video modelling, *Journal of Developmental and Physical Disabilities*, 22(4): 415–31.

Boyd, B. A., Conroy, M. A., Asmus, J. M., McKenney, E. L. W. and Mancil, G. R. (2008) Descriptive analysis of classroom setting events on the social behaviors of children with autism spectrum disorder, *Education and Training in Developmental Disabilities*, 43(2): 186–97.

Brobst, J. B., Clopton, J. R. and Hendrick, S. S. (2009) Parenting children with autism spectrum disorders: the couple's relationship, *Focus on Autism and Other Developmental Disabilities*, 24(1): 38–49.

Byers, R. (1996) Classroom processes, in B. Carpenter, R. Ashdown and K. Bovair (eds) *Enabling Access: Effective Teaching and Learning for Pupils with Learning Difficulties*. London: David Fulton.

Carr, E. G. (1985) Behavioral approaches to language and communication, in E. Schopler and G. Mesibov (eds) *Communication Problems in Autism*. London: Plenum Press.

Carr, E. G., Newsom, C. D. and Binkoff, J. (1976) Stimulus control of self-destructive behavior in a psychotic child, *Journal of Abnormal Child Psychology*, 4(2): 139–53.

Cassidy, A., McConkey, R., Truesdale-Kennedy, M. and Slevin, E. (2008) Pre-schoolers with autism spectrum disorders: the impact on families and the supports available to them, *Early Child Development and Care*, 178(2): 115–28.

Charman, T., Pellican, L., Peacey, L., Peacey, N., Forward, K. and Dockrell, J. (2011) *What is Good Practice in Autism Education?* London: Autism Education Trust.

Cheseldine, S. and Stansfield, J. (1993) *Gentle Teaching: A Guide for Carers*. Glasgow: University of Strathclyde.

Courchesne, E. (1989) Neuroanatomical subsystems involved in infantile autism: the implications of cerebellar abnormalities, in G. Dawson (ed.) *Autism: Nature, Diagnosis and Treatment*. New York: Guilford Press.

Courchesne, E. (2004) Brain development in autism, *Mental Retardation and Developmental Disabilities Research Reviews*, 10(2): 106–11.

Croen, L. A., Grether, J. K. and Selvin, S. (2002) Descriptive epidemiology of autism in a California population: who is at risk?, *Journal of Autism and Developmental Disorders*, 32(3): 217–24.

Crozier, S. and Tincani, M. (2007) Effects of Social Stories on prosocial behavior of preschool children with autism spectrum disorders, *Journal of Autism and Developmental Disorders*, 37(9): 1803–14.

Cummins, J. (1984) *Bilingualism and Special Education: Issues in Assessment and Pedagogy*. Avon: Multilingual Matters.

Currie, G. and Ravenscroft, I. (2002) *Recreative Minds*. Oxford: Clarendon Press.

Curtis, A. (1992) Overlapping dimensions: second language acquisition research and language development in autism, in G. Lowdon and P. Shattock (eds) *Living with Autism: The Individual, the Family and the Professional*. Durham: University of Durham.

D'Amour, G. and Oandasan, I. (2005) Interprofessionality as the field of inter-professional practice and interprofessional education: an emerging concept, *Journal of Interprofessional Care*, 19(Suppl. 1): 8–20.

Dale, N. (1996) *Working with Families of Children with Special Needs*. London: Routledge.

Delacato, C. (1974) *The Ultimate Stranger: The Autistic Child*. Noveto, CA: Academic Therapy Publications.

Dillenburger, K., Keenan, M., Doherty, A., Byrne, T. and Gallagher, S. (2010) Living with children diagnosed with autistic spectrum disorder: parental and professional views, *British Journal of Special Education*, 37(1): 13–23.

Drotar, D., Baskiewicz, A., Irvin, A., Kennell, J. and Klaus, M. (1975) The adaptation of parents to the birth of an infant with a congenital malformation: a hypothetical model, *Paediatrics*, 56(5): 710–17.

Dyer, K. and Luce, S. C. (1996) *Innovations: Teaching Practical Communication Skills*. Washington: American Association of Mental Retardation.

Ekas, N. V., Lickenbrock, D. M. and Whitman, T. L. (2010) Optimism, social support, and well-being in mothers of children with autism spectrum disorder, *Journal of Autism and Developmental Disabilities*, 40(10): 1274–84.

Elder, L. M., Dawson, G., Toth, K., Fein, D. and Munson, J. (2008) Head circumference as an early predictor of autism symptoms in younger siblings of children with autism spectrum disorder, *Journal of Autism and Developmental Disorders*, 38(6): 1104–11.

Estes, A., Munson, J., Dawson, G., Koehler, E., Zhou, X. and Abbott, R. (2009) Parenting stress and psychological functioning among mothers of pre-school children with autism and developmental delay, *Autism*, 13(4): 375–87.

Flippin, M., Reszka, S. and Watson, L. R. (2010) Effectiveness of the Picture Exchange Communication System (PECS) on communication and speech for children with autism spectrum disorders: a meta-analysis, *American Journal of Speech–Language Pathology*, 19(2): 178–95.

Frith, U. (1989) *Autism: Explaining the Enigma*. Oxford: Blackwell.

Frith, U. (1991) Autistic psychopathy in childhood by Hans Asperger, in U. Frith (ed.) *Autism and Asperger Syndrome*. Cambridge: Cambridge University Press.

Frith, U. (2003) *Autism: Explaining the Enigma*, 2nd edn. Oxford: Blackwell.

Frith, U. (2008) *A Very Short Introduction to Autism*. Oxford: Oxford University Press.

Fisman, S., Wolf, L., Ellison, D. and Freeman, T. (2000) A longitudinal study of siblings of children with chronic disabilities, *Canadian Journal of Psychiatry*, 45(4): 369–75.

Gillberg, C. (1991) Clinical and neurobiological aspects of Asperger syndrome in six families, in U. Frith (ed.) *Autism and Asperger Syndrome*. Cambridge: Cambridge University Press.

Goin-Kochel, R. P., Mackintosh, V. H. and Myers, B. J. (2006) How many doctors does it take to make an autism spectrum diagnosis?, *Autism*, 10(5): 439–51.

Goldiamond, I. E. (1974) Towards a constructional approach to social problems, *Behaviourism*, 2(1): 1–84.

Goodman, R. and Richards, H. (1995) Child and adolescent psychiatric presentation of second-generation Afro-Caribbeans in Britain, *British Journal of Psychiatry*, 167(3): 362–9.

Gordon, N., Pasco, G., McElduff, F., Wade, A., Howlin, P. and Charman, T. (2011) A communication-based intervention for nonverbal children with autism: what changes? Who benefits?, *Journal of Consulting and Clinical Psychology*, 79(4): 447–57.

Grandin, T. (1995) *Thinking in Pictures*. New York: Vintage Press.

Gray, C. A. (1995) Teaching children with autism to read social situations, in K. A. Quill (ed.), *Teaching Children with Autism*. New York: Delmar Publishers.

Gray, C. A. (2000) *Writing Social Stories with Carol Gray*. Arlington, TX: Future Horizons.

Gray, D. (2003) Gender and coping: the parents of children with high-functioning autism, *Social Science and Medicine*, 56(3): 631–42.

Hall, H. R. and Graff, J. C. (2010) Parenting challenges in families of children with autism: a pilot study, *Issues in Comprehensive Paediatric Nursing*, 33(4): 187–204.

Happe, F. (1999) Autism: cognitive deficit or cognitive style?, *Trends in Cognitive Sciences*, 3(6): 216–22.

Happe, F. and Frith, U. (2006) The weak central coherence account: detail-focused cognitive style in autism spectrum disorders, *Journal of Autism and Developmental Disorders*, 35(1): 5–25.

Hastings, R. P. (2006) Longitudinal relationships between sibling behavioural adjustment and behaviour problems of children with developmental disabilities, *Journal of Autism and Developmental Disorders*, 37(8): 1485–92.

Hastings, R. P., Kovshoff, H., Ward, N. J., Espinosa, F. D., Brown, T. and Remington, B. (2005) Systems analysis of stress and positive perceptions in mothers and fathers of preschool children with autism, *Journal of Autism and Developmental Disorders*, 35(5): 635–44.

Hauck, M., Fein, D., Waterhouse, L. and Feinstein, C. (1995) Social initiations by autistic children to adults and other children, *Journal of Autism and Developmental Disorders*, 25(6): 579–95.

Hill, E. L. (2004) Evaluating the theory of impairments of executive function in autism, *Developmental Review*, 24(2): 189–233.

Hobson, R. P. (1993) *Autism and the Development of Mind*. Hove: Lawrence Erlbaum Associates.

Hobson, R. P. (2002) *The Cradle of Thought*. London: Macmillan.

Hodgdon, L. A. (1995) *Visual Strategies for Improving Communication*. Michigan: Quirk Roberts Publishing.

Hodge, N. and Runswick-Cole, K. (2008) Problematising parent–professional partnerships in education, *Disability and Society*, 23(6): 637–47.

Honda, H., Shimizu, Y. and Rutter, M. (2005) No effect of MMR withdrawal on the incidence of autism: a total population study, *Journal of Child Psychology and Psychiatry*, 46(6): 572–9.

Howlin, P. (2000) Outcome in adult life for more able individuals with and without early language delays: implications for the differentiation between autism and Asperger syndrome, *Journal of Autism and Developmental Disorders*, 33(1): 3–13.

Howlin, P., Goode, S., Hutton, J. and Rutter, M. (2004) Adult outcomes for children with autism, *Journal of Child Psychology and Psychiatry*, 45(2): 212–29.

Hudry, K., Leadbitter, K., Temple, K., Slonims, V., McConachie, H., Aldred, C., Howlin, P., Charman, T. and the PACT Consortium (2010) Preschoolers with autism show greater impairment in receptive compared with expressive language abilities, *International Journal of Language and Communication Disorders*, 45(6): 681–90.

Jarrold, C. (2003) A review of research into pretend play in autism, *Autism*, 7(4): 379–90.

Jordan, R. (2003) Social play and autistic spectrum disorders, *Autism*, 7(4): 347–60.

Jordan, R. R. and Powell, S. D. (1995) *Understanding and Teaching Children with Autism*. Chichester: John Wiley and Sons.

Kaminsky, L. and Dewey, D. (2002) Psychological adjustment in siblings of children with autism, *Journal of Child Psychology and Psychiatry*, 43(2): 225–32.

Kanner, L. (1943) Autistic disturbances of affective contact, *Nervous Child*, 2: 217–50.

Kaufman, B. N. (1976) *Son-Rise*. New York: Harper and Row.

Kielinen, M., Linna, S.-L. and Moilanen, I. (2000) Autism in Northern Finland, *European Journal of Child and Adolescent Psychiatry*, 9: 162–7.

Koegel, R. L., Vernon, T. W. and Koegel, L. K. (2009) Improving social initiations in young children with autism using reinforcers with embedded social interactions, *Journal of Autism and Developmental Disorders*, 39(9): 1240–51.

Kohler, F. W., Greteman, C., Raschke, D. and Highnam, C. (2007) Using a buddy skills package to increase the social interactions between a preschooler with autism and her peers, *Topics in Early Childhood Special Education*, 27(3): 155–63.

Kok, A. J., Kong, T. Y. and Bernard-Optiz, V. (2002) A comparison of the effects of structured play and facilitated play approaches on preschoolers with autism: a case study, *Autism*, 6(2): 181–96.

Lang, R., O'Reilly, M., Healy, O., Rispoli, M., Lydon, H., Streusand, W., Davis, T., Kang, S., Sigafoos, J., Lancioni, G., Didden, R. and Giesbers, S. (2012) Sensory integration therapy for autism spectrum disorders: a systematic review, *Research in Autism Spectrum Disorders*, 6(3): 1004–18.

Lawson, J., Baron-Cohen, S. and Wheelwright, S. (2004) Empathising and systemising in adults with and without Asperger syndrome, *Journal of Autism and Developmental Disorders*, 34(3): 301–10.

Lawson, W. (2001) *Understanding and Working with the Spectrum of Autism: An Insider's View*. London: Jessica Kingsley.

Leekam, S. R., Nieto, C., Libby, S. J., Wing, L. and Gould, J. (2007) Describing the sensory abnormalities of children and adults with autism, *Journal of Autism and Developmental Disorders*, 37(5): 894–910.

Leslie, A. M. (1987) Pretense and representation: the origins of 'theory of mind', *Psychological Review*, 94(4): 412–26.

Lewis, V. and Boucher, J. (1988) Spontaneous, instructed and elicited play in relatively able autistic children, *British Journal of Developmental Psychology*, 6(4): 325–39.

Lewis, V. and Boucher, J. (1995) Generativity in the play of young people with autism, *Journal of Autism and Developmental Disorders*, 25(2): 105–21.

Lock, R. H., Hendricks, C. B., Bradley, L. J. and Layton, C. A. (2010) Using family leisure activities to support families living with autism spectrum disorders, *Journal of Humanistic Counselling, Education and Development*, 49(2): 163–80.

Lord, C., Rutter, M., DiLavore, P. and Risi, S. (2003) *Autism Diagnostic Observation Schedule*. Los Angeles: Western Psychological Services.

Lotter, V. (1966) Epidemiology of autistic conditions in young children, *Social Psychiatry*, 1(3): 124–37.

Macks, R. J. and Reeve, R. (2006) The adjustment of non-disabled siblings of children with autism, *Journal of Autism and Developmental Disorders*, 37(6): 1060–7.

Marshall, J. K. and Mirenda, P. (2002) Parent–professional collaboration for positive behaviour support at home, *Focus on Autism and other Developmental Disabilities*, 17(4): 216–28.

Medical Research Council (MRC) (2001) *MRC Review of Autism Research: Epidemiology and Causes*. London: Medical Research Council.

Mesibov, G., Shea, V. and Schopler, E. (2004) *The TEACCH Approach to Autism Spectrum Disorders*. New York: Springer.

Molyneux, J. (2001) Interprofessional team working: what makes teams work well?, *Journal of Interprofessional Care*, 15(1): 29–35.

Murdock, L. C. and Hobbs, J. Q. (2011) Picture me playing: increasing pretend play dialogue of children with autism spectrum disorders, *Journal of Autism and Developmental Disorders*, 41(7): 870–8.

Murphy, G. H., Beadle-Brown, J., Wing, L., Gould, J., Shah, A. and Holmes, N. (2005) Chronicity of challenging behaviours in people with severe intellectual disabilities and/or autism: a total population sample, *Journal of Autism and Developmental Disorders*, 35(4): 405–18.

Myles, B. S., Hagiwara, T., Dunn, W., Rinner, L., Reese, M., Huggins, A. and Becker, S. (2004) Sensory issues in children with Asperger syndrome and autism, *Education and Training in Developmental Disabilities*, 3(4): 283–90.

Nind, M. and Hewett, D. (1994) *Access to Communication: Developing the Basics of Communication with People with Severe Learning Difficulties through Intensive Interaction*. London: David Fulton.

Nissenbaum, M. S., Tollefson, N. and Reese, R. M. (2002) The interpretive conference: sharing a diagnosis of autism with families, *Focus on Autism and other Developmental Disabilities*, 17(1): 30–43.

Noens, I. and van Berckelaer-Onnes, I. (2004) Making sense in a fragmentary world: communication in people with autism and learning disability, *Autism*, 8(2): 197–218.

Nygren, G., Sandberg, E., Gillstedt, F., Ekeroth, G., Arvidsson, T. and Gillberg, C. (2012) A new screening programme for autism in a general population of Swedish toddlers, *Research in Developmental Disabilities*, 33(4): 1200–10.

O'Brien, T. (1998) *Promoting Positive Behaviour*. London: David Fulton.

Odom, S., Zercher, C., Li, S., Marquart, J., Sandall, S. and Brown, W. (2006) Social acceptance and rejection of preschool children with disabilities: a mixed-method analysis, *Journal of Educational Psychology*, 98(4): 807–23.

Orelove, F. and Sobsey, D. (1991) *Educating Children with Multiple Disabilities: A Transdisciplinary Approach*. Baltimore: Paul Brookes.

Ornitz, E. M. (1974) The modulation of sensory input and motor output in autistic children, *Journal of Autism and Childhood Schizophrenia*, 4(3): 197–215.

Owen, G., Granader, Y., Humphrey, A. and Baron-Cohen, S. (2008) LEGO® therapy and the social use of language programme: an evaluation of two social skills interventions for children with high functioning autism and Asperger syndrome, *Journal of Autism and Developmental Disorders*, 38(10): 1944–57.

Ozonoff, S. (1995) Executive functions in autism, in E. Schopler and G. B. Mesibov (eds) *Learning and Cognition in Autism*. New York: Plenum Press.

Paterson, C. R. and Arco, L. (2007) Using video modeling for generalizing toy play in children with autism, *Behavior Modification*, 31(5): 660–81.

Peeters, T. (1997) *Autism: From Theoretical Understanding to Educational Intervention*. London: Whurr.

Pennington, B. F. (2009) *Diagnosing Learning Disorders: A Neuropsychological Framework*. New York: Guilford Press.

Perepa, P. (2007) Are ASD services for minority ethnic communities accessible?, *Good Autism Practice*, 8(2): 3–8.

Perepa, P. (2008) Cultural perceptions about autism spectrum disorders and social behaviour: a qualitative study. Unpublished PhD thesis, University of Birmingham, UK.

Petalas, M. A., Hastings, R. P., Nash, S., Lloyd, T. and Dowey, A. (2009) Emotional and behavioural adjustment in siblings of children with intellectual disability with and without autism, *Autism*, 13(5): 471–83.

Phillips, N. and Beavan, L. (2012) *Teaching Play to Children with Autism*, 2nd edn. London: Sage Publications.

Piven, J., Palmer, P., Landa, R., Santangelo, S., Jacobi, D. and Childress, D. (1997) Personality and language characteristics in parents from multiple-incidence autism families, *American Journal of Medical Genetics*, 74(4): 398–411.

Plaisted, K., O'Riordan, M. and Baron-Cohen, S. (1998) Enhanced discrimination of novel, highly similar stimuli by adults with autism during a perceptual learning task, *Journal of Child Psychology and Psychiatry*, 39(5): 765–75.

Potter, C. and Whittaker, C. (2000) *Enabling Communication in Children with Autism*. London: Jessica Kingsley.

Quill, K. A. (ed.) (1995) *Teaching Children with Autism: Strategies to Enhance Communication and Socialization*. New York: Delmar Publishers.

Quintero, N. and McIntyre, L. L. (2011) Kindergarten transition preparation: a comparison of teacher and parent practices for children with autism and other developmental disabilities, *Early Childhood Education Journal*, 38(6): 411–20.

Rapin, I. and Dunn, M. (2003) Update on the language disorders of individuals on the autistic spectrum, *Brain and Development*, 25(3): 166–72.

Reese, R. M., Richman, D. M., Belmont, J. M. and Morse, P. (2005) Functional characteristics of disruptive behavior in developmentally disabled children with and without autism, *Journal of Autism and Developmental Disorders*, 35(4): 419–28.

Repp, A. C., Felce, D. and Barton, L. E. (1988) Basing the treatment of stereotypic and self-injurious behaviors on hypotheses of their causes, *Journal of Applied Behavioral Analysis*, 21(3): 281–9.

Reszka, S. S., Odom, S. L. and Hume, K. A. (2012) Ecological features of preschools and the social engagement of children with autism, *Journal of Early Intervention*, 34(1): 40–56.

Robins, D. L., Fein, D. and Barton, M. (1999) *The Modified Checklist for Autism in Toddlers (M-CHAT)*. Self-published.

Robinson, M. and Cottrell, D. (2005) Health professionals in multidisciplinary and multiagency teams: changing professional practice, *Journal of Interprofessional Care*, 19(6): 547–60.

Rogers, S., Hepburn, S. and Wehner, E. (2003) Parent reports of sensory symptoms in toddlers with autism and those with other developmental disorders, *Journal of Autism and Developmental Disorders*, 33(6): 631–42.

Russell and Harris (1993) Assessing the prevalence of aggressive behaviour and the effectiveness of interventions, in C. Kiernan (ed.) *Research into Practice?: Implications of Research on the Challenging Behaviour of People with Learning Disability*. Kidderminster: British Institute on Learning Disabilities.

Rutter, M. (2005) Aetiology of autism: findings and questions, *Journal of Intellectual Disability Research*, 49(pt 4): 231–8.

Rutter, M., Le Couteur, A. and Lord, C. (2005) *Autism Diagnostic Interview – Revised*. Los Angeles: Western Psychological Services.

Ryan, C. and Charragain, C. N. (2010) Teaching emotion recognition skills to children with autism, *Journal of Autism and Developmental Disorders*, 40(12): 1505–11.

Safer, J. (2002) *The Normal One*. New York: Bantam Dell.

Schilling, D. L. and Schwartz, I. S. (2004) Alternative seating for young children with autism spectrum disorder: effects on classroom behaviour, *Journal of Autism and Developmental Disorders*, 34(4): 423–32.

Schopler, E. and Reichler, R. J. (1983) *Individualized Assessment and Treatment for Autistic and Developmentally Disabled Children, 3: Teaching Activities for Autistic Children*. Baltimore: University Park Press.

Schreck, K. A., Williams, K. and Smith, A. F. (2004) A comparison of eating behaviors between children with and without autism, *Journal of Autism and Developmental Disorders*, 34(4): 433–8.

Sinason, V. (1992) *Mental Handicap and the Human Condition: New Approaches from the Tavistock*. London: Free Association Books.

Snyder, A., Bossomaier, T. and Mitchell, D. J. (2004) Concept formation: object attributes dynamically inhibited from conscious awareness, *Journal of Integrative Neuroscience*, 3(1): 31–46.

Stahmer, A. C. (1995) Teaching symbolic play skills to children with autism using pivotal response training, *Journal of Autism and Developmental Disorders*, 25(2): 123–41.

Stephenson, J. and Carter, M. (2009) The use of weighted vests with children with autism spectrum disorders and other disabilities, *Journal for Autism and Developmental Disorders*, 39(1): 105–14.

Sussman, F. (2004) *More Than Words*. Ontario: The Hanen Centre.

Theodorou, F. and Nind, M. (2010) Inclusion in play: a case study of a child with autism in an inclusive nursery, *Journal of Research in Special Educational Needs*, 10(2): 99–106.

Townsend, J., Harris, N. S. and Courchesne, E. (1996) Visual attention abnormalities in autism: delayed orienting to location, *Journal of the International Neuropsychological Society*, 2(6): 541–50.

Ungerer, J. A. and Sigman, M. (1981) Symbolic play and language comprehension in autistic children, *Journal of the American Academy of Child Psychiatry*, 20(2): 318–37.

Verté, S., Roeyers, H. and Buysse, A. (2003) Behavioural problems, social competence and self-concept in siblings of children with autism, *Child*, 29(3): 193–205.

Vygotsky, L. S. (1962) *Thought and Language*. Cambridge, MA: MIT Press.

Vygotsky, L. (1978) *Mind in Society: The Development of Higher Psychological Processes*. Cambridge, MA: Harvard University Press.

Wakefield, A. J., Murch, S. H., Anthony, A., Linnel, J., Casson, D. M., Malik, M., Berelowitz, M., Dhillon, A. P., Thomson, M. A., Harvey, P., Valentine, A., Davies, S. E. and Walker-Smith, J. A. (1998) Ileal-lymphoid-nodular hyperplasia, non-specific colitis, and pervasive developmental disorder in children, *The Lancet*, 351: 637–41.

Watson, L. R., Baranek, G. T. and DiLavore, P. (2003) Toddlers with autism: developmental perspectives, *Infants and Young Children*, 16(3): 201–14.

Whitaker, P. (2002) Supporting families of pre-school children with autism: what parents want and what helps, *Autism*, 6(4): 411–26.

Williams, J., Whiten, A., Suddendorf, T. and Perrett, D. (2001) Imitation, mirror neurons and autism, *Neuroscience and Biobehavioral Reviews*, 25(4): 287–95.

Wimpory, D. C., Hobson, R. P. and Nash, S. (2007) What facilitates social engagement in preschool children with autism?, *Journal of Autism and Developmental Disorders*, 37(3): 564–73.

Wing, L. (1981) Language, social and cognitive impairments in autism and severe mental retardation, *Journal of Autism and Developmental Disorders*, 11(1): 31–44.

Wing, L. (1996) *Autistic Spectrum Disorders: A Guide for Parents and Professionals*. London: Constable.

Wing, L., Leekam, S. R., Libby, S. J., Gould, J. and Larcombe, M. (2002) The Diagnostic Interview for Social and Communication Disorders: background, inter-rater reliability and clinical use, *Journal of Child Psychology and Psychiatry*, 43(3): 307–25.

Wolfberg, P. J, (2003) *Peer Play and the Autism Spectrum: The Art of Guiding Children's Socialization and Imagination*. Shawnee Mission, KS: Autism Asperger Publishing.

Wolfberg, P. J. (2009) *Play and Imagination in Children with Autism*, 2nd edn. New York: Teachers College Press and Overland Park, KS: Autism Asperger Publishing Company.

Wolfberg, P. J. and Schuler, A. L. (1993) Integrated play groups: a model for promoting the social and cognitive dimensions of play in children with autism, *Journal of Autism and Developmental Disorders*, 23(3): 467–89.

Wolpe, J. (1958) *Psychotherapy by Reciprocal Inhibition*. Stanford, CA: Stanford University Press.

Woodgate, R. L., Ateah, C. and Secco, L. (2008) Living in a world of our own: the experience of parents who have a child with autism, *Qualitative Health Research*, 18(8): 1075–83.

World Health Organization (WHO) (2007) *International Classification of Diseases*, 10th edn. Geneva: WHO.

Yirmiya, N., Erel, O., Shaked, M. and Solomonica-Levi, D. (1998) Meta-analysis comparing theory of mind abilities of individuals with autism, individuals with mental retardation, and normally developing individuals, *Psychological Bulletin*, 124(3): 283–307.

Yuill, N., Strieth, S., Roake, C., Aspden, R. and Todd, B. (2007) Designing a playground for children with autistic spectrum disorders – effects on playful peer interactions, *Journal of Autism and Developmental Disorders*, 37(6): 1192–6.

Zarkowska, E. and Clements, J. (1994) *Problem Behaviour and People with Severe Learning Disabilities*, 2nd edn. London: Chapman and Hall.

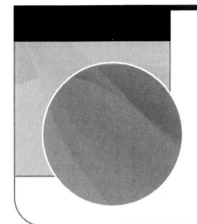

Index

Printed in Great Britain
by Amazon